Nǐ Hǎo

②

Chinese Language Course
Elementary Level

(Traditional character edition)

正體字版

by

Shumang Fredlein ● Paul Fredlein

Cheng & Tsui Company, Boston

Nǐ Hǎo 2 – Chinese Language Course
Elementary Level
(Traditional character edition)

Ni Hao 2 was first published in Australia in 1993 by ChinaSoft. The traditional character edition was first published in North America in 1999 and this revised North American edition was published in 2002 by
Cheng & Tsui Company
25 West Street
Boston, MA 02111-1213 USA
Fax (617) 426-3669
www.cheng-tsui.com
"Bringing Asia to the World"™
by arrangement with ChinaSoft Pty Ltd, Australia
Web: http://www.chinasoft.com.au

Written by Shumang Fredlein (林淑滿) & Paul Fredlein
Illustrated by Xiaolin Xue (薛曉林), Zhengdong Su (蘇正東)
Edited by Sitong Jan (詹絲桐)
Typeset by ChinaSoft on Apple Macintosh

Companion workbook, audio cassettes and CD-ROMs are also available.

ISBN 0-88727-400-5
10 9 8 7 6 5 4 3 2 1
Printed in the United States of America

Introduction

你好 Nǐ Hǎo is a basic course for beginning students of Chinese. It introduces Chinese language and culture and aims to teach communication in both spoken and written Chinese. The objectives are to enable students to use Chinese in the classroom, playground, local community and countries where the Chinese language is spoken.

The text is richly illustrated, providing a stimulating language learning tool to motivate students. Characters are used throughout the text to enhance the students' reading and writing ability. Pinyin only acts as a guide to pronunciation. When it appears on top of the characters, no capital letter is used at the beginning of the sentence and no full stop is employed. As learning progresses, the Pinyin of the characters that students have learned is omitted. To equip students to read authentic materials, various print fonts are used: Kǎishū [楷書], used in the main text, is an ideal font for students to learn to write; Sòngtǐ [宋體], used in the sentence patterns, is a font commonly used in newspapers and general publications; while Hēitǐ [黑體] is only used for titles. Apart from print fonts, various hand-written scripts are included to provide students with the opportunity to read handwriting. To make students aware of the current use of simplified characters in China, the simplified form is included in the vocabulary list in Appendix 1.

Each unit of the text in this book includes the subsections: *Illustrated texts, Learn the sentences, New words and expressions, Write the characters* and *Something to know*. In *Illustrated texts*, each conversation is based on daily life with the language in a spiralled structure. The illustrations assist in the interpretation of the conversation and are ideally suited to role playing. Grammar explanations in *Learn the sentences* are simple and illustrated with examples to clarify usage. Students can also use this section to hold conversations with partners. In *New words and expressions*, the meaning of the separate characters in each word will assist students to understand the structure of the word. Characters that the students should learn to write have the stroke order clearly illustrated in *Write the characters*. It is essential to write characters in the correct stroke order. Culture related to the content of the lesson is introduced in *Something to know*, a section designed to enrich cultural understanding and generate interest in learning the language.

In addition to the five subsections, cartoons, jokes, riddles and little stories also play important roles in the book. They are light and cheerful materials offering wonderful opportunities for practice and reinforcement.

For students who wish to learn simplified characters, the simplified character edition is published by ChinaSoft, Australia.

Contents

中國地圖
Map of China

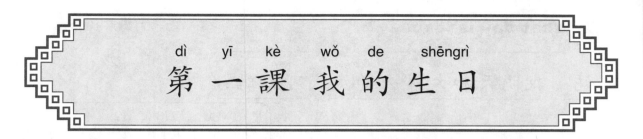

dì　yī　kè　wǒ　de　shēngrì
第 一 課 我 的 生 日

1 What is the date?

2 What day is it today?

媽，我明天和大偉去釣魚，可以嗎？
Dàwěi　diàoyú　kěyǐ

不行！明天要上學！
xíng　yào

咦！今天星期幾？
yí　xīngqí

今天星期四，明天星期五。

哦！我以為今天是星期五，明天是星期六。
ò　yǐwéi

你錯了。後天是星期六。
le　hòutiān

TUE	WED	THU	FRI	SAT
前天	昨天	今天	明天	後天

那麼，我星期六去釣魚，可以嗎？
diàoyú

也不行。你星期六要和我去買東西。
yào　mǎi

那麼星期日可以嗎？

大概可以吧！
dàgài

3 Today is my birthday

大偉，今天是五月十四日。 *Dàwěi*

我知道。今天是二〇〇二年五月十四日，星期二。 *zhīdào*

今天是我的生日，你知道嗎？ *shēngrì*

喔！真的啊！你是哪年生的？ *ō / a / nǎ / shēng*

我是一九九〇年生的。你呢？ *ne*

我也是一九九〇年生的。

你的生日是幾月幾號？

我的生日是七月十六號。

Learn the sentences

✳ **Asking the date**

To ask What's the date today? say 今天是幾號? Jīntiān shì jǐ hào? or say 今天是幾月幾
號? Jīntiān shì jǐ yuè jǐ hào? or more formally say 今天是幾月幾日？ Jīntiān shì jǐ yuè jǐ rì?
To answer, replace the question word 幾 jǐ with the number of the day and month. As 今天
jīntiān is the subject of the sentence, it is placed at the beginning. The Chinese like to use the
concept of big to small. Dates begin with the year, followed by the month and finally the day.
In spoken Chinese, the verb 是 shì is often omitted, but can be used for emphasis.

今天是幾號?	今天是二十五號。
今天幾號?	今天十九號。
今天是幾月幾號?	今天是三月七號。
今天幾月幾號?	十一月四號。
今天是幾月幾日?	今天是六月十八日。

To ask about yesterday's or tomorrow's date, replace 今天 jīntiān with 昨天 zuótiān or 明天
míngtiān. In Chinese, as tense is shown by the time stated, i.e. yesterday or tomorrow, the verb
does not change for future or past tense.

zuótiān 昨天是幾月幾號?	昨天是九月四號。
qiántiān 前天是幾月幾號?	前天是九月三號。
明天是幾月幾號?	明天是九月六號。
hòutiān 後天幾月幾號?	後天九月七號。

6

✳ **Asking the day of the week**

To ask What day is it today? say 今天是星期幾? Jīntiān shì xīngqí jǐ? To answer, replace the question word 幾 jǐ with the number of the day. The Chinese use the numbers one to six for Monday to Saturday and 天 tiān or 日 rì for Sunday. Again, the verb 是 shì, which is used in written Chinese, is often omitted in spoken Chinese, but can be used for emphasis. To ask about yesterday or tomorrow, use the same sentence structure, but replace 今天 jīntiān with 昨天 zuótiān for yesterday or 明天 míngtiān for tomorrow.

今天是星期幾?	今天是星期五。
昨天是星期幾?	昨天是星期四。
qiántiān 前天是星期幾?	前天是星期三。
明天星期幾?	明天星期六。
hòutiān 後天星期幾?	後天是星期日。
	後天星期天。

✳ **Asking the year someone was born**

To ask What year were you born? say 你是哪年生的? Nǐ shì nǎ nián shēng de? To answer, replace the question word 哪 nǎ with the number of the year.

nǎ 你是哪年生的?	我是一九六七年生的。
他是哪年生的?	他是一九五八年生的。
她是哪年生的?	她是一九八四年生的。
你姊姊是哪年生的?	她是一九七六年生的。

❈ **Confirming a date**

To ask someone to confirm a date, use 是不是 shì bú shì in the question. To answer yes, say 是 shì; to answer no, say 不是 bú shì.

今天是不是三月五日?	是。
明天是不是七月十八日?	不是。
昨天是不是十月一號?	昨天不是十月一號。

❈ **Asking if something is correct**

To ask Is it right? say 對不對 duì bú duì. To answer yes, say 對 duì; to answer no, say 不對 bú duì.

今天是五月六日，對不對?	對。
明天是五月七日，對不對?	對。
昨天是五月三日，對不對?	不對。

❈ **Seeking permission**

To ask for permission to do something, state the activity followed by 可以嗎 kěyǐ ma. To give permission, say 可以 kěyǐ. To deny permission, say 不可以 bù kěyǐ or 不行 bù xíng. In spoken Chinese, 不行 bù xíng is used more often than 不可以 bù kěyǐ.

我明天去打球，可以嗎?	可以。
我後天去游泳，可以嗎? hòutiān　yóuyǒng	不可以。
我和爸爸去釣魚，可以嗎? diàoyú	不行。

8

✳ Asking about birthdays

To ask When is your birthday? say 你的生日是幾月幾日？ Nǐ de shēngrì shì jǐ yuè jǐ rì? To answer, replace the question word 幾 jǐ with the number of the month and of the day. Another way to ask is 你的生日是什麼時候？ Nǐ de shēngrì shì shéme shíhòu?

你的生日是幾月幾日？	我的生日是二月八日。
他的生日是幾月幾號？	他的生日是十二月一號。
你哥哥的生日是什麼時候？ _{shíhòu}	他的生日是十月四日。

✳ Stating the date

To state a date, start with the year 年 nián, followed by the month 月 yuè, the day 日 rì and finally the day of the week 星期 xīngqí.

今天是一九九三年二月二十五日，星期四。
昨天是一九九三年二月二十四日，星期三。
明天是一九九三年二月二十六日，星期五。

New words and expressions

今天	jīntiān	today jīn- present (time); tiān- day, sky
月	yuè	month; the moon
號	hào	date; number
那麼	nàme	then nà- that, then (*conj.*)
昨天	zuótiān	yesterday zuó- yesterday; tiān- day, sky
明天	míngtiān	tomorrow míng- bright; tiān- day, sky
後天	hòutiān	the day after tomorrow hòu- after, behind
好了好了	hǎo le hǎo le	that's enough (to stop people from doing something)
了	le	[grammatical word] (There are many ways of using le. For details, see the explanation in Lesson 2, p. 23.)
對	duì	right, correct
錯	cuò	wrong, incorrect
釣魚	diàoyú	to fish diào- to fish with a hook and line; yú- fish
可以	kěyǐ	can, may kě- may, approve; yǐ- to use
行	xíng	all right, O.K.
要	yào	to be going to; to want
上學	shàngxué	to go to school shàng- to go to, up; xué- to study
星期	xīngqí	week xīng- star; qí- a period of time
哦	ò	oh [to indicate realization]
以為	yǐwéi	thought (mistakenly) yǐ- to use; wéi- to do
買	mǎi	to buy
日	rì	day; the sun
喔	ō	oh [to express surprise/understanding]
生	shēng	to be born, to give birth to; student
時候	shíhòu	time, moment
同	tóng	same; together
雙胞胎	shuāngbāotāi	twins shuāng- pair; bāo- born of the same parents; tāi- fetus
來	lái	[to invite someone to do something]; to come
請	qǐng	to invite; please
蛋糕	dàngāo	cake dàn- egg; gāo- cake, pudding

Days of the week

星期一	xīngqíyī	Monday
星期二	xīngqí'èr	Tuesday
星期三	xīngqísān	Wednesday
星期四	xīngqísì	Thursday
星期五	xīngqíwǔ	Friday
星期六	xīngqíliù	Saturday
星期日	xīngqírì	Sunday
星期天	xīngqítiān	Sunday

About the week

上上（個）星期	shàng shàng (ge) xīngqí	the week before last
上（個）星期	shàng (ge) xīngqí	last week
這（個）星期	zhè (ge) xīngqí	this week
下（個）星期	xià (ge) xīngqí	next week
下下（個）星期	xià xià (ge) xīngqí	the week after next

About the month

上上個月	shàng shàng ge yuè	the month before last
上個月	shàng ge yuè	last month
這個月	zhè ge yuè	this month
下個月	xià ge yuè	next month
下下個月	xià xià ge yuè	the month after next

About the day

前天	qiántiān	the day before yesterday
昨天	zuótiān	yesterday
今天	jīntiān	today
明天	míngtiān	tomorrow
後天	hòutiān	the day after tomorrow

About the year

前年	qiánnián	the year before last
去年	qùnián	last year
今年	jīnnián	this year
明年	míngnián	next year
後年	hòunián	the year after next

Write the characters

月 yuè *month; the moon*	日 rì *day; the sun*	號 hào *date, number*	今 jīn *present (time)*	明 míng *bright*
昨 zuó *yesterday*	天 tiān *day; sky*	星 xīng *star*	期 qí *a period of time*	對 duì *right, correct*
錯 cuò *wrong, incorrect*	可 kě *may, approve*	以 yǐ *to use*	行 xíng *all right, O.K.*	生 shēng *to be born, to give birth to*

everyoneloveswangli•everyoneloveswangli•everyoneloveswangli•everyoneloveswangli•everyoneloveswangli•everyoneloveswangli•everyoneloveswangli•everyoneloveswangli•everyoneloveswangli•everyoneloveswangli•everyoneloveswangli•

王 利

Wánglì
王利是一九八七年生的，今年十五

歲。他是美國人，他爸爸是中國人，媽媽
Yīngguó　　　　　Zhōngwén　de　　　tī
是英國人。王利中文說得很好。他喜歡踢
zúqiú　　　　diàoyú
足球，也喜歡釣魚。

　　　　明天是星期六，

王利要和他爸爸去
hòutiān
釣魚。後天星期日是王利的生日。王利不

喜歡他的生日；他的生日是二月二十九

日。王利有一個妹妹，今年十三歲。他妹

妹也不喜歡她的生日；她的生日是十二月

二十五日。

Something to know

❀ Chinese calendar

Since the establishment of the republic in 1912, the solar calendar has been adopted as the official calendar and all official events and holidays are practiced accordingly. However, the traditional lunar calendar, also called the agricultural calendar, is still used especially in rural areas. The lunar calendar is calculated according to the phases of the moon. A lunar month is the interval between new moons with a cycle of 29 or 30 days. There are 12 lunar months in a year with 13 months around every four years.

The calendar used today in China and Taiwan has the lunar date in small print beside the solar date, with some agricultural hints and weather indications. The current lunar month is printed on the first day of the month. The lunar dates from the first day to the 10th day have the word chū 初, which means beginning, placed before the number. From the 21st day to the 29th day, the symbol 廿, which is read as èrshí, is used instead of 二十.

二〇〇二年　二月　　　　壬午年

星期日	星期一	星期二	星期三	星期四	星期五	星期六
					1 二十	2 廿一
3 廿二	4 立春	5 廿四	6 廿五	7 廿六	8 廿七	9 廿八
10 廿九	11 三十	12 正月	13 初二	14 初三	15 初四	16 初五
17 初六	18 初七	19 雨水	20 初九	21 初十	22 十一	23 十二
24 十三	25 十四	26 十五	27 十六	28 十七		

❀ **Official holidays**

Official holidays are dated in accordance with the solar calendar. Some major celebrations are: (* public holidays)

China

*	1月　1日	New Year's Day
*	5月　1日	Labor Day
	5月　4日	Youth Day
	6月　1日	Children's Day
	9月 10日	Teacher's Day
*10月　1日		National Day

Taiwan

*	1月　1日	New Year's Day
	3月 29日	Youth Day
	4月　4日	Women & Children's Day
	9月 28日	Confucius' Birthday (Teacher's Day)
*10月 10日		National Day
	12月 25日	Constitution Day

❀ **Traditional festivals**

Although the solar calendar has been adopted as the official calendar, most Chinese traditional festivals are celebrated in accordance with the lunar calendar. The three most important festivals celebrated are the Chinese New Year, the Dragon Boat Festival and the Mid-Autumn Festival. Christmas and Easter are not widely observed except by some Christians.

1. Chinese New Year, Xīnnián 新年, first day of the first lunar month

Chinese New Year, commonly called Chūnjié 春節 (Spring Festival) or guònián 過年, is the most important and popular festival to the Chinese. During 春節, northern Chinese eat jiǎozi 餃子 (dumpling) and southern Chinese eat niángāo 年糕 (sweet cake) to celebrate the festival. Words of blessing are written on red paper, called chūnlián 春聯, and pasted on the door for good luck. Firecrackers are lit to dispel bad luck. On Chinese New Year's Eve, all family members return to the family house to have a feast called niányèfàn 年夜飯. A whole cooked fish is always placed on dinner table as the word *fish*

魚 and the verb *to spare* 餘 have the same pronunciation - yú, and so the expression niánnián yǒu yú 年年有餘, implying that one wishes there will always be something to spare every year, is represented by the presence of the fish. After dinner, the children will receive yāsuìqián 壓歲錢, money from the elder members of the family, representing the wish that they will grow well in the coming year. On New Year's Day, people dress in their best clothes to visit friends and say congratulations, gōngxǐ 恭喜 or Happy New Year, xīnnián hǎo 新年好, to each other.

Chūnjié lasts a few days and formally ends with the Lantern Festival, Yuánxiāojié 元宵節, on the 15th day of the month. Nowadays, however, most people return to work much earlier. On the night of Yuánxiāojié children carry lanterns, dēnglóng 燈籠, outdoors and people visit temples or public places to admire the lantern displays. The lantern display is a spectacular event, especially in Taiwan.

There is a legend about the origin of the New Year's celebration. Long ago, in a village, a savage beast came out of a deep forest on the last day of every year to feed on the villagers and their domestic animals. People found out that the beast was afraid of the color red and loud noises, so they pasted the red couplets, chūnlián, on the doors and lit firecrackers, biānpào 鞭炮, to scare it away.

People saying Happy New Year to each other and children lighting firecrackers

Dragon boat race

2. Dragon Boat Festival, Duānwǔjié 端午節 , fifth day of the fifth lunar month

It is said that the Dragon Boat Festival, Duānwǔjié 端午節 , is celebrated to commemorate the patriotic poet Qū Yuán 屈原 , who drowned himself in the river Mìluó Jiāng 汨羅江 , in the fourth century B.C.. Qū Yuán was an official who was exiled to a distant place by the king of Chǔ 楚 , who refused to take his suggestions. He was so disheartened that he tied himself to a rock and drowned himself in the river. People sailed their boats out to try to rescue him, but without success. They then threw rice into the river hoping that the fish would eat the rice instead of his body. The customs of dragon boat racing and eating zòngzi 粽子 , sticky rice wrapped in bamboo leaves, are believed to have originated to commemorate his death.

3. Mid-Autumn Festival, Zhōngqiūjié 中秋節 , 15th day of the eighth lunar month

This festival is also known as *the Moon Festival*. Because the lunar month starts on a new moon, it is always a full moon on this festival. On this day, people enjoy sitting outdoors admiring the full moon while eating moon cakes, yuèbǐng 月餅 , and fruits such as pomelo, yòuzi 柚子 .

Cháng'é 嫦娥 *flying to the moon after taking pills of immortality*

There is a legend that thousands of years ago, there were 10 suns in the sky and it was burning hot on earth. An archer, Hòuyì 后羿 , bravely shot down nine of the suns and saved the earth from famine. He was beloved among the people, and they made him a king. He was also awarded pills of immortality by the goddess Wángmǔ Niángniáng 王母娘娘 . The pills were for both him and his wife Cháng'é 嫦娥 , but Cháng'é was curious and could not resist the temptation of immortality. She secretly took all the pills herself, which not only made her immortal but also floated her to the moon to live forever.

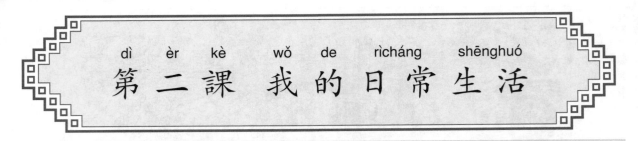

dì èr kè wǒ de rìcháng shēnghuó
第 二 課　我 的 日 常 生 活

1 What are you doing?

zài zuò
你在做什麼？

gōngkè
我在做功課。

他在做什麼？

fàng fēngzhēng
他在放風箏。

他們在做什麼？

xiàqí
他們在下棋。

kàn
他在看什麼？

mànhuà
他在看漫畫。

蘭蘭在做什麼？

我在看^{shū}書。

我在聽音樂。
tīng yīnyuè

我在寫字。
xiě zì

我在喝茶。
chá

我在跳舞。
tiàowǔ

2 What time is it?

3 What is your daily routine?

zǎoshàng　qǐchuáng
你早上幾點起床？

我七點起床。

zǎofàn
你幾點吃早飯？

我七點半吃早飯。

shàngwǔ
你上午幾點上學？

我八點二十分上學。

zhōngwǔ　　wǔfàn
你中午幾點吃午飯？

我十二點四十分吃午飯。

xiàwǔ　　fàngxué
你下午幾點放學？

我三點放學。

wǎnfàn
你幾點吃晚飯？

我六點半吃晚飯。

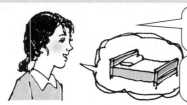

wǎnshàng　　shuìjiào
你晚上幾點睡覺？

kè
我十點一刻睡覺。

4 You are late

今天蘭蘭、大偉和小明去看九點的電影。

小明來了。

小明，你遲到了。

我遲到了？ 現在幾點？
現在差五分九點。

現在不是差五分九點。現在是
九點十分。你的錶慢了。

哦！糟糕，我的錶慢了十五分。

咦！你看，現在是九點五分
大偉，你的錶快了。

真的嗎？ 哦！我的錶快了五分。

好了！好了！我們已經遲到了。
快進去吧！

Learn the sentences

✳ **Finding out what someone is doing**

To ask What are you doing? say 你在做什麼? Nǐ zài zuò shéme? To answer, replace 什麼 shéme with the activity. The word 在 zài, which is followed by a verb, shows that the person you are asking is still doing the activity.

你在做什麼?	我在看書。 kàn shū
你在做什麼?	我在看漫畫。 mànhuà
她在做什麼?	她在聽音樂。 tīng yīnyuè
他在做什麼?	他在做功課。 gōngkè
他們在做什麼?	他們在下棋。 xiàqí

✳ **Asking the time**

To ask What's the time? say 現在幾點? Xiànzài jǐ diǎn? To state the time, start with the hour 點 diǎn, followed by the minute 分 fēn; finally, the second 秒 miǎo may also be included. Once again, the concept of big to small is seen here. Expressions such as a quarter past and a quarter to can also be used. To say a quarter past five, say 五點一刻 wǔ diǎn yí kè and to say a quarter to six, say 差一刻六點 chā yí kè liù diǎn. However, it is more common to say 15 minutes past, 十五分 shíwǔ fēn and 45 minutes past, 四十五分 sìshíwǔ fēn.

現在幾點?	現在三點。
現在幾點?	現在七點十分。
現在幾點?	現在八點一刻。 kè

現在幾點？	九點半。
現在幾點？	十點四十五分。
現在幾點？	chā 差五分十一點。
幾點了？	kuài 快十二點了。

※ **Asking what time someone does something**

To ask What time do you get up? say 你幾點起床？ Nǐ jǐ diǎn qǐchuáng? To answer, replace 幾點 jǐ diǎn with the time. This pattern can be used to ask about many activities.

你幾點起床？ qǐchuáng	我七點半起床。 bàn
你幾點上學？	我八點上學。
你幾點放學？ fàngxué	三點一刻。 kè
你幾點睡覺？ shuìjiào	我九點四十五分睡覺。

To add in the morning or in the afternoon, the phrases 早上 zǎoshàng- early morning, 上午 shàngwǔ- morning, 中午 zhōngwǔ- midday, 下午 xiàwǔ- afternoon and 晚上 wǎnshàng- evening should be placed before the time.

你早上幾點起床？ qǐchuáng	我早上七點起床。
你上午幾點上學？	我八點半上學。
你中午幾點吃午飯？	我十二點十分吃午飯。
你下午幾點放學？ fàngxué	三點半放學。
你晚上幾點睡覺？ shuìjiào	十一點。

※ **Use of** 了 le

了 le, which has no English equivalent, has many uses and can be used after a verb, an adjective or at the end of a sentence.

To confirm or emphasize a situation:	太好了！
To indicate a change in a situation:	我不吃了。 我知道了。 我會拿筷子了。 她的頭髮長了。
To indicate that the time is late:	現在幾點了？ 十點半了。 快十二點了。 我快遲到了。
To urge someone to do something or to stop someone from doing something:	該你了。 該起床了。 好了！好了！
To emphasize that something happened in the past or to indicate that something has been completed:	他來了。 我吃了。 他起床了。 昨天我的錶慢了。

New words and expressions

日常	rìcháng	day-to-day, daily rì- day; cháng- usually, often
生活	shēnghuó	life shēng- birth, life; huó- to live, alive
在	zài	[indicates an action in progress]; at, in, on
做	zuò	to do, to make
功課	gōngkè	homework, schoolwork
		gōng- effort, merit; kè- lesson, subject
放	fàng	to let off, to let go, to release
風箏	fēngzhēng	kite fēng- wind; zhēng- a Chinese string instrument
下棋	xiàqí	to play chess
看	kàn	to read, to see, to watch, to look at
漫畫	mànhuà	comic books, comic strips, cartoons
		màn- unrestrained; huà- picture, painting
聽	tīng	to listen, to hear
音樂	yīnyuè	music yīn- sound; yuè- music
寫	xiě	to write
字	zì	character, word
喝茶	hē chá	to have tea hē- to drink; chá- tea
跳舞	tiàowǔ	to dance tiào- to jump, to leap; wǔ- dance
現在	xiànzài	now, at present xiàn- now, present; zài- at
點	diǎn	o'clock; dot
分	fēn	minute
半	bàn	half
快	kuài	nearly; fast; hurry
該	gāi	should
進去	jìnqù	to go in, to enter jìn- to enter; qù- to go
早上	zǎoshàng	(early) morning zǎo- morning, early; shàng- [used after the noun to indicate scope]
起床	qǐchuáng	to get up, to get out of bed qǐ- to rise; chuáng- bed
早飯	zǎofàn	breakfast zǎo- early; fàn- meal, cooked rice
上午	shàngwǔ	morning shàng- first part, up; wǔ- noon, midday
中午	zhōngwǔ	midday, noon zhōng- middle; wǔ- noon, midday
午飯	wǔfàn	lunch wǔ- noon, midday; fàn- meal, cooked rice

下午	xiàwǔ	afternoon　xià- latter part, under; wǔ- noon, midday
放學	fàngxué	to finish classes　fàng- to let go, to release; xué- to study
晚飯	wǎnfàn	dinner　wǎn- late; fàn- meal, cooked rice
晚上	wǎnshàng	evening, night　wǎn- evening, late; shàng- [used after the noun to indicate scope]
睡覺	shuìjiào	to sleep　shuì- to sleep; jiào- sleep
刻	kè	a quarter (of an hour)
電影	diànyǐng	movie　diàn- electricity; yǐng- shadow, image
遲到	chídào	to arrive late　chí- late; dào- to arrive
差	chā	differ from
錶	biǎo	watch (timepiece)
慢	màn	slow; slowly
糟糕	zāogāo	[oral] oh no; how terrible zāo- in a wretched state; gāo- cake
已經	yǐjīng	already
零	líng	zero (in written form)

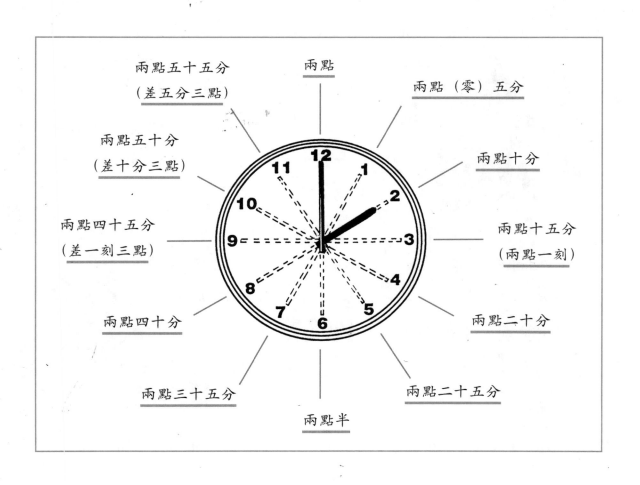

Write the characters

在	做	看	書	寫
zài [in progress]; at, in, on	zuò to do, to make	kàn to read, see, watch	shū book	xiě to write
字	現	點	分	半
zì character, word	xiàn now, present	diǎn o'clock; dot	fēn minute	bàn half
了	下	午	早	晚
le [grammatical word]	xià latter part; under	wǔ noon, midday	zǎo morning, early	wǎn evening, late

everyoneloveswangli•everyoneloveswangli•everyoneloveswangli•everyoneloveswangli•everyoneloveswangli•everyoneloveswangli•everyoneloveswangli

妹 妹 呢 ？

王利和他妹妹都喜歡寵物。王利
Wánglì　　　　　　　*dōu*

有一隻大狗和兩隻小鳥。他妹妹有一隻
　　　　　　　　niǎo

小貓和五條金魚。
māo　　*tiáo jīnyú*

今 天 是 星 期 天 。

早上王利五點半起床，五點三十五分去跑步，
　　　　　　　qǐchuáng　　　　　　　　　*pǎobù*

七點吃早飯，七點半和爸爸下棋。現在是九點
　　　　　　　　　　　　xiàqí

一刻，王利在看漫畫，他爸爸在喝茶，
kè　　　　*mànhuà*　　　　*hē chá*

他媽媽在聽音樂。王利的妹妹呢? 她在
　　　tīng yīnyuè　　　　　　　*ne*

做什麼?

Something to know

❀ **Chinese tea**

Tea is important in the daily life of the Chinese people. Tea contains caffeine, pigmentation, aromatic oils, vitamins, minerals and protein. People drink tea both at home and at work to quench their thirst, to refresh themselves and to aid digestion. Tea is also used as a medicine, in cooking and as a sacrificial offering. There are many varieties, which can generally be divided into three categories according to the method of manufacture: green tea, black tea and wulong tea. Green tea is unfermented; black tea is fully fermented and wulong tea is half fermented. There is also flower-scented tea with jasmine tea being the most popular. Every type of tea has its own characteristics.

There are two ways in which the Chinese enjoy tea: one is drinking, and the other is tasting. Weaker tea is drunk for refreshment and to quench the thirst. Strong tea is for tasting. The tea set for tasting consists of a small tray shaped like a shallow bowl, a small tea pot and four small cups. Each tea cup holds around 15 to 20 ml of tea, and the teapot makes just enough to fill the four cups. The tray is filled with hot water after the tea is made so as to keep the tea warm. In order to savor the quality, people drink tea slowly and with appreciation.

❁ Traditional leisure activities

Some Chinese children's games such as rope skipping, shuttlecock kicking, kite flying and top spinning have a long history. Chinese chess, xiàngqí 象棋, the "go" game, wéiqí 圍棋, and mahjong, májiàng 麻將, are also popular leisure activities. Xiàngqí and wéiqí are both games for two people. The aim of xiàngqí is to take the opposition's general, and the aim of wéiqí is to encircle more territory than that held by the opposition. Májiàng is played by four people and is popular among those who have plenty of leisure time. Because playing májiàng is very time-consuming, somewhat engrossing and sometimes used for gambling, some people object to it.

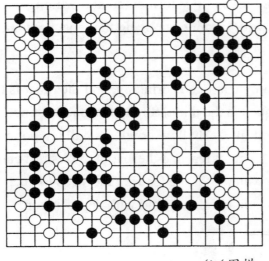

wéiqí 圍棋

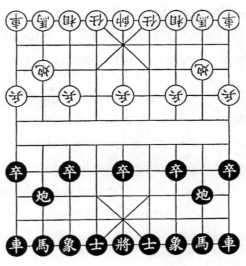

xiàngqí 象棋

❁ Daily routine of Chinese students

In China, students arrive at school early. Teams of students take turns sweeping up the leaves on the school grounds early in the morning. In high school, zhōngxué 中學, students still have most of the lessons in their homeroom as in elementary school. There are around 50 students in each class. The duration of the lesson is normally 45 minutes each with a 10-minute recess in between. Group physical exercise, which is normally held in the morning, is a daily routine. At some schools, eye exercises are also held each day to relax the eye muscles. At lunchtime, most of the students go home to have lunch. In Taiwan, students do not leave school during the lunch break, but take a short nap at their desks to refresh themselves for the afternoon lessons.

Apart from their curriculum subjects, students can choose to attend extracurricular activities, which may be held one or two afternoons each week. After cleaning the classroom at the end of the day, some students make their way home and some head for the Children's Palace, Shàoniángōng 少年宮. Children's Palaces are found in most cities in China to provide gifted students aged between seven and seventeen with specialized training in arts, science or sports.

dì　sān　kè　　Xiǎomíng　de　jiā
第 三 課 小 明 的 家

1 Where are they?

　　小明家有六個人。他有爸爸、媽媽、一個哥哥、
一個姊姊和一個弟弟。他家還有一隻小貓和一隻小
狗。現在他們都在哪兒?

　　弟弟在車子上面;爸爸在車子下面。媽媽在車子
前面;小明在車子後面。姊姊在車子右邊;哥哥在
車子左邊。小狗在車子裡面;小貓在車子外面。

2 House plan

這是小明的家。小明的家在蘭蘭家對面。蘭蘭
家是公寓。小明家是洋房。小明家前面是花園，
後面有一個游泳池。房子左邊是陽台，下面是車庫。

Dream home!

　　小明家有兩間<ruby>臥室<rt>jiān wòshì</rt></ruby>、一間<ruby>書房<rt>shūfáng</rt></ruby>、一間<ruby>客廳<rt>kètīng</rt></ruby>和一間<ruby>飯廳<rt>fàntīng</rt></ruby>。<ruby>另外<rt>lìngwài</rt></ruby><ruby>還<rt>hái</rt></ruby>有<ruby>廚房<rt>chúfáng</rt></ruby>、<ruby>洗衣房<rt>xǐyīfáng</rt></ruby>、<ruby>廁所<rt>cèsuǒ</rt></ruby>和<ruby>浴室<rt>yùshì</rt></ruby>。客廳在<ruby>最<rt>zuì</rt></ruby>前面。飯廳在客廳後面。兩間臥室在客廳右邊。書房在臥室後面。洗衣房、廁所和浴室在<ruby>最<rt>zuì</rt></ruby>後面。

3 What happened?

媽，我回來了。
huílái

放學了？
fàngxué

是啊！都快四點了。
a　　dōu kuài

咦！怎麼回事？
yí　　zěme　huí shì
我們的沙發不見了。
shāfā　　jiàn

沙發太舊了，我們買了
tài jiù　　　　mǎi
一套新的，明天送來。
tào xīn　　　　sòng lái

我們的電視機也不見了。
diànshìjī

電視機壞了，送去修理了。
huài　　sòng　xiūlǐ

4 Xiaoming's Sunday

今天是星期日。小明今天很早起床，很晚睡覺。
（qǐchuáng）（shuìjiào）

早上五點，他在游泳池游泳。
（yóuyǒng chí）

上午十點半，他在客廳沙發上睡覺。
（kètīng shāfā）

中午十二點，他在廚房打太極拳。
（chúfáng tàijíquán）

下午兩點，他在洗衣房唱歌。
（xǐyīfáng chànggē）

下午六點，他在浴室裡打電話。
（yùshì diànhuà）

晚上七點，他在電視機前面吃飯。
（diànshìjī）

晚上九點，他在書房看漫畫。
（shūfáng mànhuà）

半夜十二點，他在客廳做功課。
（bànyè kètīng gōngkè）

Learn the sentences

❋ **Asking the location of something**

To state a location, for example on top of the car, say 在車子上面 zài chēzi shàngmiàn. In this example, the word 上面 shàngmiàn, indicating the location, should follow the object 車子 chēzi to which it relates. The word order is the opposite of the English example.

chēzi 在車子上面	在車子下面
diànbīngxiāng 在電冰箱前面	在電冰箱後面
diànshìjī 在電視機左邊	在電視機右邊
chēkù 在車庫裡面	在車庫外面

To state the location of someone or something, for example My shoes are on top of the car, say 我的鞋子在車子上面。Wǒ de xiézi zài chēzi shàngmiàn. To change this sentence into a question, replace the location 車子上面 chēzi shàngmiàn with the question word 哪兒 nǎr or 哪裡 nǎlǐ. The sentence becomes 我的鞋子在哪兒？Wǒ de xiézi zài nǎr? or 我的鞋子在哪裡？Wǒ de xiézi zài nǎlǐ?

xiézi 我的鞋子在哪兒？	chēzi 你的鞋子在車子上面。
我的書在哪裡？	shāfā 你的書在沙發下面。
shūfáng 你的書房在哪兒？	kètīng 在客廳後面。
cèsuǒ 你們的廁所在哪裡？	zuì 在最後面。
小明在哪裡？	wòshì 他在臥室。
大偉，你在哪兒？	chúfáng 我在廚房。

In spoken Chinese, we can use 呢 ne instead of 在哪裡 zài nǎlǐ or 在哪兒 zài nǎr to ask where someone or something is.

我的鞋子呢？ *xiézi ne*	在電冰箱上面！ *diànbīngxiāng*
我的書呢？	我怎麼知道？ *zhīdào*
我們的電視機呢？ *diànshìjī*	壞了，送去修理了。 *huài sòng xiūlǐ*

✳ Asking what someone is doing somewhere

In Lesson 2, we learned how to ask what someone is doing. For example, the question 他在做什麼？ Tā zài zuò shéme? and the reply 他在看電視。Tā zài kàn diànshì. To add the *somewhere*, place the location of the activity before the verb. To say *He is watching TV in the living room*, say 他在客廳看電視。Tā zài kètīng kàn diànshì.

他在客廳做什麼？ *kètīng*	他在客廳看電視。 *diànshì*
他在書房做什麼？ *shūfáng*	他在書房做功課。 *gōngkè*
他在飯廳做什麼？ *fàntīng*	吃飯。

✳ Asking where someone is doing something

To ask *where someone is doing something*, use the previous pattern but replace the location with the question word 哪裡 nǎlǐ or 哪兒 nǎr. The sentence 他在客廳看電視。Tā zài kètīng kàn diànshì. becomes 他在哪裡看電視？ Tā zài nǎlǐ kàn diànshì? or 他在哪兒看電視？ Tā zài nǎr kàn diànshì?

他在哪兒看電視？ *diànshì*	他在客廳看電視。 *kètīng*
他在哪裡睡覺？ *shuìjiào*	他在沙發上睡覺。 *shāfā*
他在哪兒吃飯？	他在電視機前面吃飯。 *diànshìjī*

✻ **Asking what happened**

To ask What happened? or What's the matter? say 怎麼回事？ Zěme huí shì? Here, 回 huí is a measure word for 事 shì.

怎麼回事？	我們的電視機壞了。 diànshìjī huài
這是怎麼回事？	我們的車子壞了。 chēzi
這是怎麼回事？	你的水床破了。 shuǐchuáng pò

✻ **Finding out where someone sleeps**

We have learned that to ask Where do I sleep? 我在哪兒睡覺？ Wǒ zài nǎr shuìjiào? which is a formal expression. In spoken Chinese, it is more common to say 我睡哪兒？ Wǒ shuì nǎr?

你昨天晚上睡哪兒？ shuì	睡客廳地板。 kètīng dìbǎn
你今天晚上睡哪兒？	睡我弟弟的床。 chuáng
你明天晚上睡哪兒？	睡客廳沙發。 shāfā

New words and expressions

還	hái	also, still
在	zài	at, in, on; [indicating an action in progress]
哪兒	nǎr	[oral] where, also said as 哪裡 nǎlǐ nǎ- where, which, what; (é)r- [a word ending]
車子	chēzi	car, vehicle
上面	shàngmiàn	on top of, above shàng- up, above; miàn- [word ending - location], face
下面	xiàmiàn	under, below xià- down, under
前面	qiánmiàn	front qián- front, before
後面	hòumiàn	behind hòu- behind, after
右邊	yòubiān	right (location) yòu- right
左邊	zuǒbiān	left (location) zuǒ- left; biān- [word ending - location], side
裡面	lǐmiàn	inside lǐ- inside
外面	wàimiàn	outside wài- outside
對面	duìmiàn	opposite (location) duì- opposite, correct
公寓	gōngyù	apartments; (multi-story building – 樓房 lóufáng)
洋房	yángfáng	Western-style house; (single-story house – 平房 píngfáng) yáng- foreign, ocean; fáng- house; píng- flat, level
花園	huāyuán	garden huā- flower; yuán- garden, park
游泳池	yóuyǒng chí	swimming pool yóuyǒng- to swim; chí- pool, pond
房子	fángzi	house
陽台	yángtái	balcony, veranda yáng- the sun; tái- platform
車庫	chēkù	garage chē- vehicle; kù- storehouse, storage
間	jiān	[a measure word for room]
臥室	wòshì	bedroom wò- to lie down; shì- room
書房	shūfáng	study shū- book; fáng- room, house
客廳	kètīng	living room kè- guest; tīng- hall
飯廳	fàntīng	dining room fàn- meal, cooked rice; tīng- hall
另外	lìngwài	in addition, besides
廚房	chúfáng	kitchen chú- kitchen; fáng- room, house
洗衣房	xǐyīfáng	laundry xǐ- to wash; yī- clothes; fáng- room, house
廁所	cèsuǒ	restroom, lavatory, also said as 洗手間 xǐshǒujiān in Taiwan cè- restroom, lavatory; suǒ- place; xǐ- to wash; shǒu- hand; jiān- room
浴室	yùshì	bathroom, shower room yù- to bathe; shì- room

最	zuì	most
回來	huílái	to come back, to return　huí- to return; lái- to come
都	dōu	already; all
怎麼回事	zěme huí shì	what happened; what's the matter　zěme- what, why; huí- [a measure word for matter]; shì- affair, matter
沙發	shāfā	sofa (transliteration of sofa)
見	jiàn	to see, to catch sight of
太	tài	too (exceedingly)
舊	jiù	old (nonliving things), worn
套	tào	[a measure word for clothing or furniture], set, suit
新	xīn	new
送	sòng	to deliver, to send
送來	sòng lái	to deliver or send to (here)　lái- to come
電視機	diànshìjī	television set　diànshì- television; jī- machine
壞	huài	broken down; bad
送去	sòng qù	to deliver or send to (there)　qù- to go
修理	xiūlǐ	to repair, to fix　xiū- to repair; lǐ- to put in order
洗衣機	xǐyījī	washing machine　xǐ- to wash; yī- clothes; jī- machine
電冰箱	diànbīngxiāng	refrigerator　diàn- electricity; bīng- ice; xiāng- box
天哪	tiān na	Good heavens!　tiān- sky, heaven; na- [a word ending]
水床	shuǐchuáng	water bed　shuǐ- water; chuáng- bed
破	pò	broken, torn
倒霉	dǎoméi	to have bad luck　dǎo- upside down; méi- mould
睡	shuì	to sleep
唉	ài	(a sigh)
地板	dìbǎn	floor　dì- floor, ground; bǎn- board
早	zǎo	early
晚	wǎn	late
打	dǎ	to play (ball game, taichi etc); to dial (telephone)
太極拳	tàijíquán	taichi
唱歌	chànggē	to sing, singing　chàng- to sing; gē- song
電話	diànhuà	telephone　diàn- electricity; huà- speech
半夜	bànyè	midnight　bàn- half; yè- night, evening
鞋子	xiézi	shoes
電視	diànshì	television　diàn- electricity; shì- to look at, sight
謎語	míyǔ	riddle　mí- mystery; yǔ- language
猜	cāi	to guess

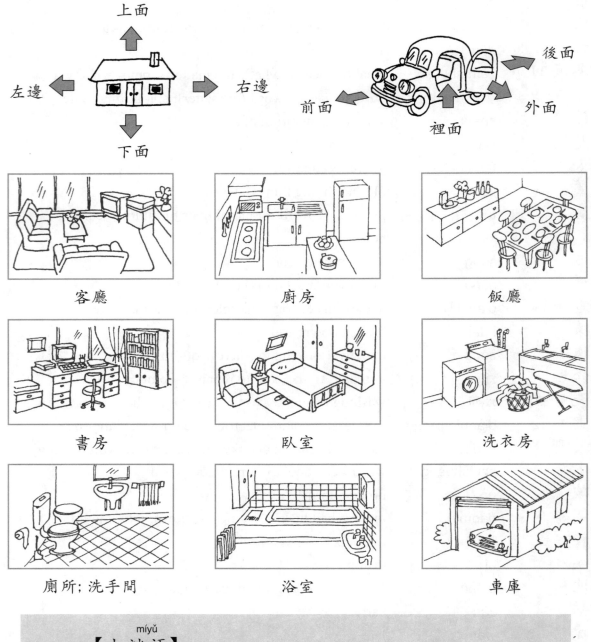

上面

左邊   右邊

下面

後面

前面   外面

裡面

客廳   廚房   飯廳

書房   臥室   洗衣房

廁所; 洗手間   浴室   車庫

【小謎語】 míyǔ

1. 兩個人。（猜一字）cāi

2. 生日。（猜一字）

3. 九天加一天。（猜一字）jiā

4. 家裡沒有動物，也沒有大人。（猜一字）

Write the characters

哪	兒	前	面	後
nǎ *where; which; what*	ér *[word ending]*	qián *front, before*	miàn *[word ending]; face*	hòu *behind, after*
右	邊	左	裡	外
yòu *right (location)*	biān *[word ending]; side*	zuǒ *left (location)*	lǐ *inside*	wài *outside*
回	來	怎	事	見
huí *to return; [measure word]*	lái *to come*	zěn *how*	shì *matter, business*	jiàn *to see*

家

王利的家很大，前面是游泳池（yóuyǒng chí），後面有一個大花園（huāyuán）。王利的臥室（wòshì）在左邊最（zuì）後面，浴室（yùshì）和廁所（cèsuǒ）在他房間（fángjiān）右邊。

今天晚上，王利一家人七點半吃晚飯。他爸爸在車庫（chēkù）裡吃，媽媽在廚房（chúfáng）裡吃，妹妹在臥室（wòshì）裡吃，王利在書房裡吃。吃了晚飯，王利一家人都在客廳（kètīng）：王利在聽音樂（tīng yīnyuè），妹妹在唱歌（chànggē），爸爸在看電視（diànshì），媽媽在看書。

Something to know

❀ Housing

Because of the high population density, the traditional U-shaped Chinese house, called sìhéyuàn 四合院, has almost disappeared except for a few places in the country. The U-shaped house, surrounding a court yard, was usually made of mud bricks, with some luxurious ones being built of clay bricks. The room in which ancestors were worshipped was in the center of the house. More rooms could be added behind the two wings of the U-shaped building, which made it an ideal house for the traditionally large family consisting of grandparents, aunts and uncles, parents, children and grandchildren. In the 20th century, because of the emergence of the nuclear family, apartments have become the main form of housing, especially in urban areas.

In the city in China, housing is traditionally provided by government employers, called dānwèi 單位. Workers lease their apartments from their dānwèi for a very low rent. The apartment usually contains small rooms and the restroom is often shared by a few families. To save room, people often use the little veranda for cooking as well as for drying clothes. There are apartments containing better facilities for more affluent people, but they are not numerous. In recent years, a private housing policy has been introduced, and people are being encouraged to buy their own apartments.

In the country, many families still have three generations living together, that is, grandparents, parents and children. After 1978, the commune system was dismantled, and agricultural production returned to being based on the family unit. A "free market" was established for farmers to earn extra money from selling surplus grain, fruit, vegetables and chickens. Some peasants have become wealthy compared to those who live in the city and earn a salary. They can afford to build their own houses or even two- or three-story mansions equipped with better and more modern electrical facilities.

In Taiwan, the standard of living is similar to that of the West. Due to the high population density and the scarcity of land, people in the cities mainly live in high-rise buildings. However, there are still traditional U-shaped houses in country areas, although they are also disappearing, to be replaced with multi-story buildings.

sìhéyuàn 四合院

dì　sì　kè　wǒ　de　yīfú
第四課　我的衣服

1 | What clothes do they wear?

chuān　　　　yīfú
他們穿什麼衣服？

Wáng xiānshēng chuān hēsè   xīzhuāng
王先生穿黑色的西裝。
tàitai   lǜsè   yángzhuāng
王太太穿綠色的洋裝。

Lǐ   bái chènshān   lán kùzi
李老師穿白襯衫、藍褲子。
zǐ   qípáo
白小姐穿紫旗袍。

hóng mián'ǎo
小妹妹穿紅棉襖。
                          xù
小弟弟穿白色的 T 恤、
kāfēisè   duǎnkù
咖啡色的短褲。

qiǎn huángsè   máoyī
蘭蘭穿淺黃色的毛衣、
shēn   qúnzi   chéngsè
深黃色的裙子和橙色
wàitào
的外套。

2 Do they fit?

jiàn chènshān　cháng
這件襯衫太長了；

duǎn
那件襯衫太短了。

tiáo qúnzi　　kuān
這條裙子太寬了；

zhǎi
那條裙子太窄了。

tào xīzhuāng
這套西裝太大了；

那套西裝太小了。

qípáo　　qǐlái　　héshēn
這件旗袍穿起來很合身。

xù　　　　shūfú
那件T恤穿起來很舒服。

mián'ǎo　　　shímáo
這件棉襖看起來很時髦。

yángzhuāng　　piàoliàng
那件洋裝看起來很漂亮。

3 What should I wear?

媽，今天是小明的生日。
我該(gāi)穿哪件衣服呢(ne)？

穿那件綠色的洋裝(yángzhuāng)吧！

那件洋裝太窄(zhǎi)了，不好看。

那麼，那件藍色的呢？

那件太長(cháng)了我不喜歡。

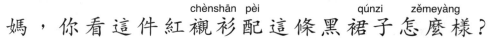

媽，你看這件紅襯衫(chènshān)配(pèi)這條黑裙子(qúnzi)怎麼樣(zěmeyàng)？

啊(a)！挺時髦(tǐng shímáo)，挺好看的。

4 Where are my shoes?

不是這雙。這雙是舊的。
我在找新的。

新的？客廳裡找找吧！

找到了。在電視機上面。

哦……時髦嘛！

小明，看看你的襪子，一隻
是白的，一隻是黑的。

Learn the sentences

※ **Asking what someone is wearing**

To ask what clothes someone is wearing, use 穿什麼衣服 chuān shéme yīfú. This is often shortened to 穿什麼 chuān shéme. To answer, replace this phrase with a description of the clothes being worn.

他今天穿什麼衣服？	他穿黃襯衫、黑褲子。 chènshān　kùzi
她今天穿什麼？	她穿藍旗袍。 qípáo
她昨天穿什麼？	她穿綠色的洋裝。 yángzhuāng

※ **Describing how clothes fit**

When describing something using 太 tài- too, 了 le is usually used after the stative verb. For example, to say too big, say 太大了 tài dà le. However, to use phrases such as not too, the 了 le is not used. Therefore, to say not too big, say 不太大 bú tài dà.

這雙皮鞋太大了。 shuāng píxié	那雙皮鞋太小了。
這條裙子太寬了。 tiáo qúnzi kuān	那條裙子太窄了。 zhǎi
我的褲子太長了。 kùzi cháng	你的褲子太短了。 duǎn
這件衣服不太大。	那件毛衣不太小。 máoyī

※ **Use of 起來 qǐlái after the verb**

The meaning of 起來 qǐlái is literally to stand up, to rise. However, it can be used after a verb to express an impression or an opinion of something.

那件衣服穿起來很合身。

這件衣服穿起來真不舒服。

你的棉襖看起來很漂亮。

她的洋裝看起來很時髦。

這個漢堡看起來不好看，吃起來很好吃。

✳ Wondering what to wear

To ask Which clothes should I wear? say 我該穿哪件衣服呢? Wǒ gāi chuān nǎ jiàn yīfú ne?
Here, 該 gāi means should.

我明天該穿哪件衣服呢?	穿那件紫旗袍吧！
我今天該穿哪件衣服呢?	穿那套藍色的西裝吧！
我明天該穿哪雙皮鞋呢?	穿那雙黑色的吧！

✳ Asking for an opinion

To ask an opinion from someone on something, use 怎麼樣 zěmeyàng, which means how about or what about. To say How about this? or What about this? say 這個怎麼樣? Zhè ge zěmeyàng?

這個怎麼樣?	很好。
這件衣服怎麼樣?	很好看。
那雙皮鞋怎麼樣?	穿起來很舒服。
這條裙子怎麼樣?	太寬了。

The verb 看 kàn, literally meaning to see, can be used to ask an opinion and is equivalent to to think. Therefore, 你看怎麼樣？ Nǐ kàn zěmeyàng? means What do you think?

你看這件棉襖怎麼樣？ (mián'ǎo)	很漂亮。 (piàoliàng)
你看這件襯衫怎麼樣？ (chènshān)	我看太大了。

✳ **Use of** 有沒有 yǒu méi yǒu **before a verb**

We have learned to use 有沒有 yǒu méi yǒu to ask whether someone has something, i.e. 你有沒有哥哥？ Nǐ yǒu méi yǒu gēge? In this situation, 有沒有 yǒu méi yǒu is used before a noun. It can also be used before a verb to indicate an inquiry as to whether something has happened in the past. This usage is particularly common in Taiwan. To say Did you have breakfast? say 你有沒有吃早飯？ Nǐ yǒu méi yǒu chī zǎofàn?

你有沒有看到我的鞋子？ (kàndào)　(xiézi)	有，在沙發下面。 (shāfā)
你今天有沒有吃早飯？	沒有。
你昨天有沒有去游泳？ (yóuyǒng)	我沒有去。

People wearing the traditional clothing chángpáo mǎguà 長袍馬掛
acting the comic dialogue xiàngshēng 相聲

New words and expressions

衣服	yīfú	clothes, clothing yī- clothes; fú- clothes
穿	chuān	to wear (clothes, shoes or socks)
王	Wáng	a surname wáng- king
先生	xiānshēng	Mr.; (in Taiwan) husband xiān- first; shēng- born
黑色	hēisè	black hēi- black; sè- color
西裝	xīzhuāng	Western-style attire, suit xī- west; zhuāng- outfit
太太	tàitai	Mrs.; (in Taiwan) wife tài- too
綠色	lǜsè	green lǜ- green; sè- color
洋裝	yángzhuāng	woman's dress, called 連衣裙 liányīqún in China yáng- foreign; zhuāng- outfit; lián- to join; yī- clothes; qún- skirt
白	bái	white
襯衫	chènshān	shirt
藍	lán	blue
褲子	kùzi	trousers, pants
小姐	xiǎojiě	Miss.; young lady
紫	zǐ	purple
旗袍	qípáo	a close-fitting dress with a high neck and a slit skirt
紅	hóng	red
棉襖	mián'ǎo	cotton-padded coat
白色	báisè	white bái- white; sè- color
T恤	T-xù	T-shirt hàn- sweat; shān- shirt
咖啡色	kāfēisè	brown kāfēi- (transliteration of coffee); sè- color
短褲	duǎnkù	shorts duǎn- short; kù- pants, trousers
淺	qiǎn	light (color); shallow
黃色	huángsè	yellow huáng- yellow; sè- color
毛衣	máoyī	sweater máo- fur, feather; yī- clothes
深	shēn	dark (color); deep
裙子	qúnzi	skirt
橙色	chéngsè	orange (color) chéng- orange; sè- color
外套	wàitào	coat wài- outside; tào- cover
件	jiàn	[a measure word for clothing or affair]
條	tiáo	[a measure word for trousers, skirt, river, belt etc.]
寬	kuān	loose-fitting (clothing), (肥 féi is used in China); wide
窄	zhǎi	tight-fitting (clothing), (瘦 shòu is used in China); narrow
穿起來	chuān qǐlái	impression or feeling of the clothes on someone

合身	héshēn	well-fitting (clothing)	hé- fit; shēn- body
舒服	shūfú	comfortable	shū- comfortable; fú- comfortable, clothes
看起來	kàn qǐlái	looks, impression or feeling of the look	
時髦	shímáo	fashion, fashionable	
漂亮	piàoliàng	pretty	piào- pretty; liàng- bright, shinning
配	pèi	to match	
怎麼樣	zěmeyàng	how about, what about	zěnme- how, what; yàng- appearance
挺	tǐng	[oral] very	
好看	hǎokàn	good-looking	
雙	shuāng	[a measure word for shoes, socks, gloves etc.] pair	
皮鞋	píxié	leather shoes	pí- leather; xié- shoes
怎麼	zěme	how, what	
自己	zìjǐ	self	
找找	zhǎozhǎo	to have a look for	zhǎo- to look for
找	zhǎo	to look for	
看到	kàndào	to catch sight of, to see	kàn- to see; dào- to reach
好像	hǎoxiàng	seem, be like	hǎo- good; xiàng- alike
冰箱	bīngxiāng	refrigerator	bīng- ice; xiāng- box
旁邊	pángbiān	the side	
找到了	zhǎodào le	found	zhǎo- to look for; dào- to reach, to arrive
看看	kànkàn	to have a look	kàn- to see, to look
襪子	wàzi	socks	
隻	zhī	[a measure word for animal or single shoe and sock]	
嘛	ma	[word ending, indicates an obvious situation]	

（件）西裝　（件）襯衫　（件）T恤　（件）毛衣　（件）外套　（件）棉襖　（件）旗袍

（件）洋裝　（條）褲子　（條）短褲　（條）裙子　（雙）（隻）皮鞋　（雙）（隻）襪子

Write the characters

穿 chuān *to wear*	衣 yī *clothes*	服 fú *clothes*	先 xiān *first*	太 tài *too (exceedingly)*
黑 hēi *black*	白 bái *white*	紅 hóng *red*	黃 huáng *yellow*	藍 lán *blue*
綠 lǜ *green*	色 sè *color*	件 jiàn *[measure word]*	呢 ne *[question word]*	找 zhǎo *to look for*

everyoneloveswangli•everyoneloveswangli•everyoneloveswangli•everyoneloveswangli•everyoneloveswangli•everyoneloveswangli•everyoneloveswangli•everyoneloveswangli•everyoneloveswangli

太 時髦 了
shímáo

王利的妹妹有很多衣服：襯衫、裙子、
chènshān　qúnzi
毛衣、外套、洋裝；白色的、黑色的、紅色
máoyī　wàitào　yángzhuāng
的、黃色的、藍色的、綠色的，很多很多。
今天她不知道該穿哪件衣服，她說：「這條
zhīdào gāi　　　　　　　　　　　tiáo
太長了，那條太短了⋯⋯這件太寬了，那件
cháng　　　duǎn　　　　　　kuān
太窄了⋯⋯這條太舊
zhǎi　　　　　　jiù
了，那條太新了⋯⋯
xīn
這件太合身了，那件
héshēn
太時髦了⋯⋯」
shímáo

Something to know

🏵 Traditional clothes today

Some clothing worn by the Chinese today still retains the Mandarin style of the Qing dynasty, but with some modifications. Qípáo 旗袍 and mián'ǎo 棉襖 are the two most popular styles. Qípáo is a close-fitting dress with a high neck and a slit skirt. It is still regarded as women's formal dress. Mián'ǎo is a cotton-padded jacket. The softness and warmth of the jacket makes it ideal for the cold winter. Chángpáo mǎguà 長袍馬掛, a mandarin jacket worn over a gown by men, is no longer everyday wear but is worn on the stage, particularly by those who perform xiàngshēng 相聲, a comic dialogue (see the drawing on page 50). The best material for this clothing is silk.

A style, in white, worn by Dr. Sun Yat-sen called Zhōngshānzhuāng 中山裝, was once popular, and the style, in blue, worn by Nikolai Lenin called Lièníngzhuāng 列寧裝 became popular in China after China became a communist country in 1949 and is still worn today by some people.

🏵 Chinese silk

Silk cloth in China dates back to the Neolithic period, around 7,000 to 1,600 B.C.. Silk is produced from the cocoons of silkworms, which are raised on woven trays and fed with hand-picked mulberry leaves. Before the moths emerge, the cocoons are plunged into boiling water and the silk fiber is reeled off. With care, the fiber can be reeled off in a continuous unbroken thread to an average length of around 1600 feet. The silk fiber is then used to produce a luxurious textile. Silk is light, soft, smooth and durable.

In the early days, silk was the favorite textile of the imperial family and was often used as gifts for rulers of other countries. The Silk Road, a route from China to overseas, was gradually formed due to the export of silk to Japan and to the West. Today, silk is still one of the main exports of China. The embroidery of Sūzhōu 蘇州, called sūxiù 蘇繡, and that of Húnán 湖南, called xiāngxiù 湘繡, are world famous.

🏵 Chinese colors

Traditionally, Chinese regarded white as the color of mourning and red as the color of luck. Before the influence of the West and the popularity of the white wedding dress in the 20th century, Chinese brides wore red wedding dresses. Yellow is particularly associated with the emperor. The garment of the emperor was described as the *Yellow Robe*, Huángpáo 黃袍, which is normally decorated with the dragon. Gold, the color of wealth, green, the color of prosperity, and red were used for the decorations of the imperial palace and are still widely used in many Taoist temples in Taiwan.

dì　wǔ　kè　mǎi　dōngxī
第 五 課 買 東 西

---

1 **How much is it?**

圖	句子	價錢	讀法
	shuāng　xiézi　duōshǎo qián 這雙鞋子多少錢？	65.00	kuài 六十五塊
	tiáo　kùzi 這條褲子多少錢？	37.00	三十七塊
	dǐng　màozi 這頂帽子多少錢？	4.50	四塊半
	jiàn yángzhuāng 這件洋裝多少錢？	78.50	七十八塊五
	xiāngjiāo　　　　jīn 香蕉多少錢一斤？	1.30	一塊三
	júzi　　　　dài 橘子多少錢一袋？	3.80	三塊八
	fènglí 鳳梨多少錢一個？	1.05	líng 一塊零五分
	cǎoméi　　mài 草莓怎麼賣？	2.85	máo　　jīn 兩塊八毛五一斤
	lìzhī 荔枝怎麼賣？	1.49	一塊四毛九一斤

2 In the department store

小明今天要到百貨公司買東西。
<ruby>要<rt>yào</rt></ruby> <ruby>到<rt>dào</rt></ruby> <ruby>百貨<rt>bǎihuò</rt></ruby> <ruby>公司<rt>gōngsī</rt></ruby> <ruby>買<rt>mǎi</rt></ruby> <ruby>東西<rt>dōngxī</rt></ruby>

他的書包壞了。他想買個新的。
<ruby>書包<rt>shūbāo</rt></ruby> <ruby>壞<rt>huài</rt></ruby> <ruby>新<rt>xīn</rt></ruby>

請問，你們這兒賣書包嗎？
<ruby>請問<rt>qǐngwèn</rt></ruby> <ruby>書包<rt>shūbāo</rt></ruby>

賣。這個好不好？

這個很好，可是我不要綠色的。
<ruby>要<rt>yào</rt></ruby>

有沒有藍色的？

有。這個怎麼樣？
<ruby>怎麼樣<rt>zěmeyàng</rt></ruby>

3 In the bookshop

大偉今天到書店買東西。

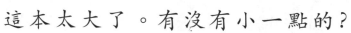

4 At the market

Learn the sentences

✳ **Asking the price**

To ask how much (money), say 多少錢 duōshǎo qián. To state an amount of money, use the measure words 塊 kuài for dollars, 毛 máo for ten-cent units and 分 fēn for cents from one to nine. In spoken Chinese, the last measure word 分 fēn is not normally said, but to avoid confusion, 分 must be said if there are no ten-cent units. For example, to say ¥5.30, say 五塊三 wǔ kuài sān, to say ¥5.03, say 五塊零三分 wǔ kuài líng sān fēn. When the amount of money ends in 50 cents, 半 bàn can be used to indicate half a dollar, or simply use 五.

這本字典多少錢？ zìdiǎn	兩塊。
這件衣服多少錢？	十五塊七。
這頂帽子多少錢？ dǐng màozi	八塊六毛九。
這雙皮鞋多少錢？ shuāng píxié	七十五塊半。

¥1.00: 一塊/元 yuán   ¥0.10: 一毛/角 jiǎo   ¥0.01: 一分

¥0.50: 五毛/角   ¥1.50: 一塊半 or 一塊五

To ask the price of something by item, pairs or weight, place the measure word before or after 多少錢 duōshǎo qián. To ask How much each? say 一個多少錢？ Yí ge duōshǎo qián? or 多少錢一個？ Duōshǎo qián yí ge?

多少錢一斤？ jīn	一斤多少錢？
多少錢一個？	一個多少錢？
香蕉多少錢一斤？ xiāngjiāo	香蕉一斤多少錢？
報紙多少錢一份？ bàozhǐ　　fèn	報紙一份多少錢？
雜誌多少錢一本？ zázhì	雜誌一本多少錢？

Another way to ask about price is to use 怎麼賣 zěme mài, which means *how is (it) sold*. The reply may be ¥3.00 a bag 一袋三塊 yí dài sān kuài or perhaps 50 cents each 一個五毛 yí gè wǔ máo.

píngguǒ 蘋果怎麼賣？	jīn 一斤一塊三。
fènglí 鳳梨怎麼賣？	一個八毛。
júzi 橘子怎麼賣？	dài 一袋兩塊五。

✳ Asking if something is for sale

To ask *Do you sell school bags?* say 你們賣書包嗎？ Nǐmen mài shūbāo ma? The reply for yes is 賣 mài and for no 不賣 bú mài. Alternatively, ask *Do you have school bags?* 你們有書包嗎？ Nǐmen yǒu shūbāo ma?

shūbāo 請問，你們賣書包嗎？	賣。
zìdiǎn 請問，你們賣字典嗎？	duìbùqǐ 對不起，我們不賣。
請問，你們有書包嗎？	有。你要哪個？
dìtú 請問，你們有地圖嗎？	對不起，我們沒有。

＊ **Expressing an opinion on goods or asking for a choice**

> 這件棉襖還不錯，可是太貴了。
> _{mián'ǎo} _{guì}
>
> 這件襯衫挺好的，可是太大了。
> _{chènshān tǐng}
>
> 這件毛衣太貴了，有沒有便宜一點的？
> _{piányí}
>
> 這雙皮鞋太大了，有沒有小一點的？
> _{shuāng píxié}
>
> 這葡萄太酸了，有沒有甜一點的？
> _{pútáo suān} _{tián}
>
> 我不要藍色的，有沒有綠色的？

＊ **Asking whether something is sweet or sour**

To ask whether something is sweet, use 甜不甜 tián bù tián; for sour, use 酸不酸 suān bù suān.

蘋果甜不甜？	很甜。
鳳梨甜不甜？	非常甜。
橘子酸不酸？	不太酸。
葡萄酸不酸？	一點都不酸。

＊ **Stating degree**

extremely	very	not very	not	not at all
非常甜	很甜	不太甜	不甜	一點都不甜
非常酸	很酸	不太酸	不酸	一點都不酸

✳ **Use of 的 de**

1. 的 can be used after a noun, a pronoun, an adjective or a verb to form an attribute to modify the word that follows it. The word being modified can be omitted if it is previously mentioned or is obviously known.

after a noun/pronoun (possessive):	姊姊的書；姊姊的 我的衣服；我的
after a noun/pronoun (modifying):	紅色的襯衫^{chènshān}；紅色的 九點的電影^{diànyǐng}；九點的
after a conditional verb:	昨天買的蘋果^{píngguǒ}；昨天買的 要去打球的人；要去打球的 一九八四年生的人；一九八四年生的
after an adjective:	紅的襯衫；紅的 新的皮鞋^{píxié}；新的 便宜一點^{piányí}的書包^{shūbāo}；便宜一點的 小一點的字典^{zìdiǎn}；小一點的 *(When the adjective is a single character, 的 is often omitted, e.g. 紅襯衫，新皮鞋)*

2. 的 used in spoken form:

used after 挺^{tǐng}:	挺好的，挺漂亮^{piàoliàng}的
used for emphasis:	真的 (Really?/Really!)
used to soften a reply:	是－是的；好－好的

New words and expressions

多少	duōshǎo	how much, how many
		duō- many, much, more; shǎo- few, little, less
錢	qián	money
塊	kuài	[oral] monetary unit for dollars, formally called 元 yuán
頂	dǐng	[a measure word for hat, cap]; top
帽子	màozi	hat, cap
香蕉	xiāngjiāo	banana　xiāng- fragrant; jiāo- a broadleaf plant
斤	jīn	a unit of weight = 0.6 kg in Taiwan = 0.5 kg in China
橘子	júzi	tangerine, mandarin
袋	dài	bag
鳳梨	fènglí	pineapple, called 菠蘿 bōluó in China
分	fēn	a unit of money, cent (= 0.01 元 yuán or 塊 kuài)
草莓	cǎoméi	strawberry　cǎo- straw; méi- berry
賣	mài	to sell
毛	máo	[oral] 10-cent unit (= 0.1 元 yuán), formally called 角 jiǎo
荔枝	lìzhī	lychee
百貨公司	bǎihuò gōngsī	department store　bǎi- one hundred; huò- goods; gōngsī- company
可是	kěshì	but, however
要	yào	to want; to be going to
還不錯	hái búcuò	[oral] not bad, pretty good　bù- not; cuò- wrong
貴	guì	expensive
便宜	piányí	cheap, inexpensive
一點	yìdiǎn	a little　yī- one; diǎn- dot, o'clock
給	gěi	to give
找	zhǎo	to make change; to look for
您	nín	[polite form] you
書店	shūdiàn	bookshop　shū- book; diàn- shop
地圖	dìtú	map　dì- ground; tú- picture
那	nà	[conjunction] then, shorten from 那麼 nàme
字典	zìdiǎn	dictionary　zì- word; diǎn- record, book

本	běn	[a measure word for books, magazines and dictionaries]
漢英字典	Hàn-Yīng zìdiǎn	Chinese-English dictionary
		Hàn- China, name of a dynasty; Yīng- English
雜誌	zázhì	magazine zá- miscellaneous; zhì- record, annals
份	fèn	[a measure word for newspapers, copies]
報紙	bàozhǐ	newspaper bào- to report; zhǐ - paper
一共	yígòng	all together yī- one; gòng- together
市場	shìchǎng	market shì- market; chǎng- place
水果	shuǐguǒ	fruit shuǐ- water; guǒ- fruit
蘋果	píngguǒ	apple
甜	tián	sweet
葡萄	pútáo	grape
酸	suān	sour
一點都不	yìdiǎn dōu bù	not at all yìdiǎn- a little; dōu- all; bù- not
非常	fēicháng	extremely fēi- not; cháng- usually, often
串	chuàn	[a measure word for grapes or bananas] bunch, cluster
元	yuán	[formal] monetary unit for dollar, also written as 圓
角	jiǎo	[formal] 10-cent unit

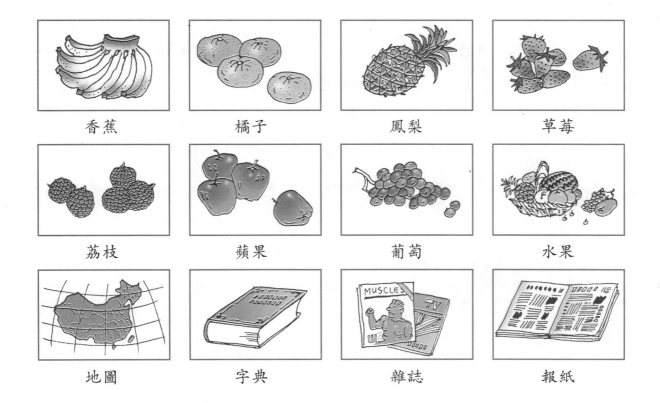

香蕉	橘子	鳳梨	草莓
荔枝	蘋果	葡萄	水果
地圖	字典	雜誌	報紙

Write the characters

多	少	錢	買	賣
duō *many, much, more*	shǎo *few, little, less*	qián *money*	mǎi *to buy*	mài *to sell*
塊	毛	到	樣	還
kuài *dollar*	máo *10-cent unit*	dào *to arrive, to go to*	yàng *appearance*	hái *also; still*
要	給	謝	本	共
yào *to want; to be going to*	gěi *to give*	xiè *to thank*	běn *[measure word]*	gòng *together*

everyoneloveswangli•everyoneloveswangli•everyoneloveswangli•everyoneloveswangli•everyoneloveswangli•everyoneloveswangli•everyoneloveswangli•everyoneloveswangli•everyoneloveswangli•everyoneloveswangli

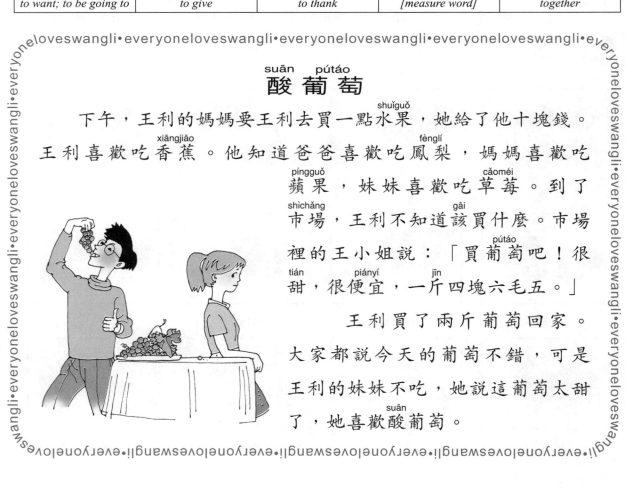

酸 葡萄
suān pútáo

下午，王利的媽媽要王利去買一點水果，她給了他十塊錢。
王利喜歡吃香蕉（xiāngjiāo）。他知道爸爸喜歡吃鳳梨（fènglí），媽媽喜歡吃
蘋果（píngguǒ），妹妹喜歡吃草莓（cǎoméi）。到了
市場（shìchǎng），王利不知道該（gāi）買什麼。市場
裡的王小姐說：「買葡萄（pútáo）吧！很
甜（tián），很便宜（piányí），一斤（jīn）四塊六毛五。」

王利買了兩斤葡萄回家。
大家都說今天的葡萄不錯，可是
王利的妹妹不吃，她說這葡萄太甜
了，她喜歡酸（suān）葡萄。

Something to know

🌸 The currencies in China and Taiwan

The currency used in China is called rénmínbì 人民幣, *people's money*, and the monetary symbol is ¥. The currency used in Taiwan is called xīntáibì 新台幣, *new currency of Taiwan*, and the monetary symbol is $. The numbers used on notes and coins are in a complicated form, i.e. 壹(一)、貳(二)、參(三)、肆(四)、伍(五)、陸(六)、柒(七)、捌(八)、玖(九)、拾 (十). Cheques are also written in this form so they cannot be easily altered. Commodity prices in China, although varying at times, are generally much lower than in Australia or in America.

Notes and coins used in China

Notes and coins used in Taiwan

🌸 Department stores and markets

Chinese people like fresh food, so most people buy what they need in the market every day. Apart from local markets, there are also shops and department stores. In Taiwan, all shops are privately run. In China, most department stores are operated by the goverment because of the communist system. Prices in these stores are fixed, and no bargaining is practiced. However, many free markets are now privately run, and fruit, fish, meat, live chickens and groceries are sold, and bargaining is normally practiced as in some markets in Taiwan.

A scene in a free market

dì liù kè bàifǎng péngyǒu
第 六 課 拜 訪 朋 友

1 Inviting

2 Visiting

星期六……

3 Introducing

4 Leaving

時間不早了。我該走了。
shíjiān　　gāi

媽！大偉要走了。

阿姨我走了。謝謝您的招待。
āyí　　　　　　zhāodài

在這兒吃晚飯嘛！
ma

不用了。謝謝您。
yòng
今天太打擾您了。
dǎrǎo

不用客氣，有空常來玩。
yòng kèqì　　　cháng

謝謝你，小明，今天游泳真過癮。
yóuyǒng guòyǐn

下星期日再來吧！
zài

太打擾了吧？
dǎrǎo

不會。我們都歡迎你來。可以嗎？
dōu huānyíng

行。下星期日我再來。

 **Learn the sentences**

✳ **Asking if someone is available**

To ask if someone is available, use either 有空嗎 yǒu kòng ma or 有沒有空 yǒu méi yǒu kòng. To answer yes, say 有 yǒu; to answer no, say 沒有 méi yǒu. 沒有 méi yǒu is often shortened as 沒 méi in a statement, e.g. 我沒空 Wǒ méi kòng.

你明天有空嗎?	沒有。
你今天下午有空嗎?	有。
你後天有沒有空?	我後天沒空。
你星期天有空嗎?	對不起，我沒空。 duìbùqǐ
你九月十三日有空嗎?	有啊！有什麼事嗎?

✳ **Asking where someone lives**

To ask Where do you live? say 你住在哪裡? Nǐ zhù zài nǎlǐ? The 在 zài is optional in oral conversation. To answer, replace the question word 哪裡 nǎlǐ with the place name.

你住在哪裡?	我住在芝加哥。 Zhījiāgē
他住哪裡?	他住紐約。 Niǔyuē
你爸爸住在哪裡?	他住在舊金山。 Jiùjīnshān
你媽媽住在哪裡?	她住在雪梨。 Xuělí

✳ **Asking someone's telephone number**

To ask someone's telephone number, use 幾號 jǐhào. To answer the question, replace 幾號 jǐhào with the number. In China, it is more common to use 多少 duōshǎo than 幾號 jǐhào.

你家的電話號碼是幾號？ （hàomǎ）	我家的電話是三七八五六六五。
你家的電話是幾號？	五六九六四六四。
他家的電話是幾號？	他家電話是八九〇一二三四。
她家的電話是幾號？	好像是六四〇五五三三。 （hǎoxiàng）

✳ Asking where someone works

To ask Where do you work? say 你在哪裡工作？ Nǐ zài nǎlǐ gōngzuò? To answer the question, replace 哪裡工作 nǎlǐ gōngzuò with the place and type of work.

你在哪裡工作？	我在中學教書。 （jiāoshū）
你爸爸在哪裡工作？	他在銀行上班。 （yínháng shàngbān）
他在哪裡工作？	他在白宮上班。 （Báigōng）
你姊姊在哪裡工作？	她是護士，在醫院上班。 （hùshì yīyuàn）

✳ Asking if someone is home

To ask if someone is home, use either 在家嗎 zài jiā ma or 在不在家 zài bú zài jiā. To reply yes to the question, say 在 zài; to reply no, say 不在 bú zài.

請問他在家嗎？	他在。
請問他在不在？	他不在。
你媽媽在家嗎？	在，我去叫她。
你弟弟在不在家？	在，你等一下，我去叫他。
你明天在不在家？	在啊！有什麼事嗎？ （a）

✳ **Use of** 一下 yíxià

一下 yíxià is sometimes used after a verb to indicate that action is short in duration. To say wait a minute or wait a while say 等一下 děng yíxià.

請你等一下，我馬上回來。

來，我給你們介紹一下。
　　　　jièshào

給我看一下，可以嗎?

✳ **Polite expressions used when visiting**

Expressions a host uses when a visitor arrives:	
歡迎你來。 huānyíng	謝謝。
吃飯了嗎?	吃了，謝謝。
Expressions a host uses when a visitor is leaving:	
有空常來玩。 　　cháng	好。
慢走。 màn	
Expressions a visitor uses when leaving:	
謝謝您的招待。 　　　zhāodài	不要客氣。 　　kèqì
太打擾您了。 　dǎrǎo	哪裡，不用客氣。 　　　　yòng

【小笑話】
　xiàohuà

　　王太太在她家門口和李太太談話，談了兩個小時。
　Wáng　　　　　　ménkǒu　Lǐ　tánhuà

王先生問她:「你為什麼不請李太太進來坐?」

王太太回答:「李太太說她沒有時間。」
　　　huídá

New words and expressions

拜訪	bàifǎng	to visit
空	kòng	free time, spare time
玩	wán	to play, to have fun wán- to play
錄影帶	lùyǐngdài	video, video cassette lù- to record; yǐng- image; dài- cassette
住	zhù	to live
寫下來	xiě xiàlái	to write down xiě- to write; xiàlái- to come down
皇后	huánghòu	queen
街	jiē	street
號碼	hàomǎ	number hào- number, date; mǎ- code
哪位	nǎ/něi wèi	which one (person) 哪 is often pronounced as něi when directly followed by a measure word
位	wèi	respectful measure word for people
等	děng	to wait
一下	yíxià	a short while
等一下	děng yíxià	to wait a moment
馬上	mǎshàng	right away mǎ- horse; shàng- on, up
出來	chūlái	to come out chū- to go or to come out; lái- to come
介紹	jièshào	to introduce
叔叔	shúshu	a form of address for a man of about one's father's age; father's younger brother
阿姨	āyí	a form of address for a woman of about one's mother's age; (in southern China) mother's sister
矽谷	Xìgǔ	Silicon Valley xì- silicon; gǔ- valley
父親	fùqīn	father

工作	gōngzuò	to work, work
舊金山	Jiùjīnshān	San Francisco　jiù- old; jīn- gold; shān- mountain
上班	shàngbān	to go to work　shàng- to go to, up; bān- duty, class
母親	mǔqīn	mother
中學	zhōngxué	high school (primary school – 小學 xiǎoxué, university – 大學 dàxué)
教書	jiāoshū	to teach (at school)　jiāo- to teach; shū- book
時間	shíjiān	(concept of) time　shí- hour; jiān- within
走	zǒu	to leave, to go
招待	zhāodài	to receive (guests); reception
不用	búyòng	need not　bù- not; yòng- to use
打擾	dǎrǎo	to disturb, to trouble
常	cháng	often
過癮	guòyǐn	to one's heart's content, fully enjoyed
再	zài	again
會	huì	will; can, be able to
事	shì	thing, business; matter
芝加哥	Zhījiāgē	Chicago
紐約	Niǔyuē	New York
雪梨	Xuělí	Sydney (said as 悉尼 Xīní in China)
銀行	yínháng	bank　yín- silver; háng- business, firm
白宮	Báigōng	the White House　bái- white; gōng- palace
醫院	yīyuàn	hospital
慢走	mànzǒu	to walk slowly and take care
笑話	xiàohuà	joke　xiào- to laugh; huà- speech, talk
門口	ménkǒu	doorway　mén- door; kǒu- mouth
談話	tánhuà	to have conversation, to talk, to chat
談	tán	to talk, to chat
小時	xiǎoshí	hour (time duration)
問	wèn	to ask
為什麼	wèishéme	why
進來	jìnlái	to come in　jìn- to enter; lái- to come
坐	zuò	to sit
回答	huídá	to answer　huí- to return; dá- to answer
說	shuō	to say

Write the characters

空 kòng *free time*	玩 wán *to play, to have fun*	住 zhù *to live*	電 diàn *electricity*	話 huà *speech*
請 qǐng *please; to invite*	問 wèn *to ask*	進 jìn *to enter*	等 děng *to wait*	出 chū *to come/go out*
時 shí *time, hour*	間 jiān *within; [measure word]*	該 gāi *should*	走 zǒu *to go, to leave, to walk*	再 zài *again*

everyoneloveswangli·everyoneloveswangli·everyoneloveswangli·everyone

馬上回來

星期六上午十一點，林朋去找王利，可是王利不在家。王利的妹妹在家。她說王利和媽媽去百貨公司(bǎihuò gōngsī)買一雙(shuāng)皮鞋(píxié)，馬上回來。她請

林朋進去客廳(kètīng)坐(zuò)，也請他喝茶(chá)。林朋介紹(jièshào)他自己(zìjǐ)，說他是王利的同班同學(tóngbān)，住在學校對面，他父親(fùqīn)和母親(mǔqīn)都(dōu)在學校(xuéxiào)教書(jiāoshū)。

下午三點，林朋說他該走了。王利的妹妹說：「你再等一下，王利馬上回來。」

Something to know

✿ Addressing friends' parents

It is considered rude to call older people by their names in Chinese society. There are polite forms of address, which vary from place to place. The most common forms used by children to address their friends' parents or parents' friends are shúshu 叔叔 and āyí 阿姨. Shúshu is a term used for the younger brothers of the father, but is used here to address males of one's parents' generation, while āyí is used for females. In some areas, bóbo 伯伯, a term for the father's older brother, and bómǔ 伯母, a term for his wife, are used if the person looks obviously much older than one's parents. In Taiwan and in some southern areas, the surname followed by māma 媽媽 is often used for married females.

✿ Open your gift?

When visiting, it is common for the guest to present a gift to the host. This gift can be a cake, a basket of fruit, or a little toy for the children. However, it is a Chinese custom that the host does not unwrap the present in front of the visitor as this is regarded as impolite. The host is expected to welcome the visitor, but not to be looking forward to receiving presents. Although most overseas Chinese have adopted the Western custom of unwrapping presents as soon as they are received, those who have recently come from China or Taiwan still tend to maintain tradition.

✿ Would you like a cup of coffee?

During a formal visit, if the host asks the guest: Would you like a cup of coffee? Yào bú yào hē bēi kāfēi 要不要喝杯咖啡? the reply will normally be no, bú yào 不要, even if the guest is hot and thirsty. Chinese regard saying I would love to, wǒ yào 我要, as impolite. Saying no means that the guest does not want to cause the host too much trouble. Chinese drink tea at home rather than coffee. Normally, the host will offer the guest some tea, a cold drink, or fruit without asking.

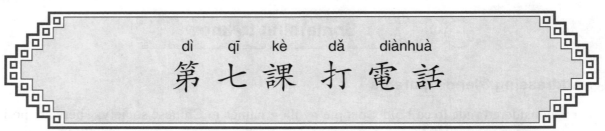

1 A wrong number

2 Not home

三九七四二五八。　喂！
請問是三九七四二五八嗎？

是。您找誰？

wéi
喂！

Lǐ
我找李蘭蘭。請問她在不在家？

蘭蘭不在家。您是哪位？

wèi

我是蘭蘭的同學。我叫白大偉。
shíhòu
請問，蘭蘭什麼時候回來？

Měiyí　　yóuyǒng
蘭蘭和美怡去游泳了，
下午三點左右回來。

Lǐ shúshu
那我下午再打來。您是李叔叔？

再見，李叔叔。

是的。

再見。

3 Wait a moment, please

wéi
喂！

喂！李叔叔好！我是白大偉。

大偉，你好。你找蘭蘭？

是的。她回來了嗎？

回來了。你等一會兒，我去叫她。

好的。謝謝您。

蘭蘭！你的電話。你的同學白大偉找你。

好，我馬上來。

yìhuǐr
你等一會兒，蘭蘭馬上來。

好的。謝謝您，李叔叔。

4 Speaking

喂！是蘭蘭嗎？
wéi

喂！

是啊，我就是。
有什麼事嗎，大偉？
a jiù

你明天可以和我一起去中國城嗎？
chéng

你要去中國城做什麼？

我想去買一雙功夫鞋。
shuāng gōngfū xié

你喜歡功夫鞋啊？

是啊！功夫鞋穿起來很舒服。
shūfú

好吧！可是我明天沒空，後天可以嗎？

後天也可以。

幾點鐘？
zhōng

中午十二點可以嗎？，我來接你。
jiē

沒問題。後天見。
wèntí

Learn the sentences

✻ **Asking who is speaking on the telephone**

To ask Who is speaking? say 您是哪位? Nín shì nǎ/něi wèi? To answer, say your name or your relationship to the person being sought.

您是哪位?	我是小王。 (Wáng)
您是哪位?	我是蘭蘭的同學。
您是哪位?	我是李叔叔。
請問您是哪位?	我是王阿姨。 (āyí)

✻ **Asking someone who he/she is looking for**

To ask Who are you looking for? say 你找誰? Nǐ zhǎo shéi? or more politely say 您找哪位? Nín zhǎo nǎ/něi wèi? To answer, replace 誰 shéi or 哪位 nǎ/něi wèi with the person's name or title.

你找誰?	我找白太太。
您找哪位?	我找李太太。
您找哪位?	我找林老師。 (Lín)

✽ **Asking to talk to someone on the telephone**

To ask to speak to a certain person on the telephone, ask whether the person is home. For example, in Lesson 6, we learned to ask Is Lanlan home? say 蘭蘭在家嗎? Lánlán zài jiā ma? or 蘭蘭在不在家? Lánlán zài bú zài jiā? Alternatively, we can say 我找蘭蘭 Wǒ zhǎo Lánlán, which means I'm looking for Lanlan.

我找大偉。	我就是。 (jiù)
我找蘭蘭。請問她在不在?	她在。我去叫她。
我找美怡。請問她在家嗎? (Měiyí)	她不在。您是哪位?
我找小明。請問他在家嗎?	對不起，你打錯號碼了。 (hàomǎ)

✽ **Asking if someone has come back**

To ask Has he come back? say 他回來了嗎? Tā huílái le ma? To answer yes, say 他回來了。 Tā huílái le. To answer no, say 他還沒回來。 Tā hái méi huílái. Notice the use of 了 le for a completed action as learned in Lesson 2.

請問，林老師回來了嗎? (Lín)	他回來了。
大偉回來了嗎?	他還沒回來。
你哥哥回來了嗎?	回來了。
你妹妹回來了嗎?	還沒。

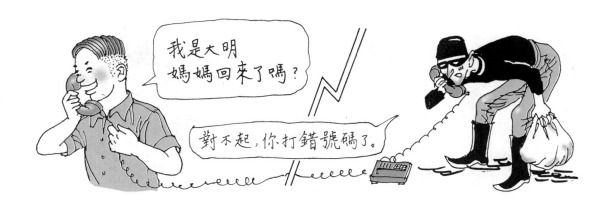

✱ **Asking when someone is coming back**

To ask When are you coming back? say 你什麼時候回來？ Nǐ shéme shíhòu huílái? when both the time and day are required. If only the time is needed, say 你幾點回來？ Nǐ jǐ diǎn huílái?

他幾點回來？	他十點左右回來。
你媽媽幾點回來？	她下午兩點半回來。
你什麼時候回來？ shíhòu	明天上午九點。
你爸爸什麼時候回來？	他九月二十五回來。

✱ **Asking someone the purpose of going somewhere**

To ask someone the purpose of going somewhere use 去 qù + v. + 什麼 shéme.

你要去中國城做什麼？	去買一雙功夫鞋。
你要去紐約做什麼？ Niǔyuē	去找朋友。
你要去舊金山做什麼？ Jiùjīnshān	去玩。
你要去書店買什麼？ shūdiàn	去買一本字典。 zìdiǎn
你去百貨公司買什麼？ bǎihuò gōngsī	去買一條褲子。 tiáo kùzi

說錯話了

今天是老王的生日，他請了很多人去他家吃飯，時間是中午十二點。①

唉！快十二點了！為什麼該來的人還不來？②

該來的人還不來！那麼，我們是不該來的人啦！走了，我們走了。③

咦！為什麼不該走的人走了？④

不該走的人走了！那麼，我們是該走的人啦！走，我們走了。⑤

老王！你說錯話了。大家都以為你不歡迎他們。

我說錯話了？我不歡迎的不是他們。⑥

你不歡迎的不是他們！那麼，你不歡迎的是我啦！我走了！再見！⑦

New words and expressions

喂	wéi; wèi	hello (on the telephone); hey
鈴	líng	(telephone ringing sound); bell
左右	zuǒyòu	around, approximately zuǒ- left; yòu- right
一會兒	yìhuǐr	a little while
我就是	wǒ jiù shì	I am (the person)
一起	yìqǐ	together
中國城	Zhōngguóchéng	Chinatown Zhōngguó- China; chéng- town
功夫鞋	gōngfū xié	Chinese soft shoes originally the footwear of the martial arts gōngfū- martial arts; xié- shoes
幾點鐘	jǐ diǎn zhōng	what time zhōng- clock
接	jiē	to meet, to pick (someone) up
沒問題	méi wèntí	no problems
說話	shuōhuà	to speak
老王	Lǎo Wáng	Old Wang (Used to address an older friend whose surname is Wang) lǎo- old; wáng- a surname, king
啦	la	[exclamation]
入口	rùkǒu	entrance rù- to enter; kǒu- mouth
出口	chūkǒu	exit chū- to go out; kǒu- mouth
推	tuī	to push
拉	lā	to pull
男廁	náncè	men's restroom nán- male; cè- restroom
女廁	nǚcè	women's restroom nǚ- female

Signs in Chinatown

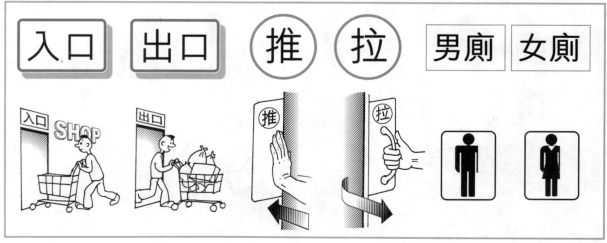

Write the characters

偉 wěi *great*	蘭 lán *orchid*	起 qǐ *to rise*	您 nín *you [polite form]*	李 Lǐ; lǐ *a surname; plum*
位 wèi *[measure word]*	叔 shū *one's father's younger brother*	候 hòu *time*	游 yóu *to swim*	泳 yǒng *swim*
城 chéng *town*	雙 shuāng *pair*	功 gōng *skill*	夫 fū *man*	鞋 xié *shoes*

對 不 起

　　今天王利有空，他想找林朋到他家玩。上午十點半，他打電話給林朋，接（jiē）電話的是林朋的爸爸。他說林朋去中國城（chéng）買東西（dōngxī），下午一點半左右回來。下午兩點，王利再打電話，接（jiē）電話的是林朋的姊姊。她說林朋去買報紙（bàozhǐ），馬上回來。三點一刻（kè），王利再打電話，接電話的是林朋的妹妹。她說林朋在廁所（cèsuǒ），請他等一下。三點四十分，林朋接了電話，他說：「對不起，王利，時間不早了，我不去你家了。」

Something to know

❀ Chinatown and Chinese migrants

The huge number and the wide dispersion of Chinese migrants is reflected in the saying "Where the sea reaches, there Chinese can be found". Chinese language is commonly used and the old customs are practiced by overseas Chinese. This can be seen particularly in the Chinatowns in the big cities of many countries such as the United States, Canada, Japan and Australia. In Chinatown, Zhōngguóchéng 中國城, or sometimes called Tángrénjiē 唐人街, namely Chinese street, there are Chinese grocery stores, medicine shops, restaurants, gift shops etc.

Chinese migration dates back to 540 A.D., with around 7,000 families residing in Japan at that time. Most migrants left China after the 16th century, when Chinese laborers were transported by some Western countries to their colonies as coolies. Many people on the southeast coast of China, where the land is poor, moved to southeast Asia to seek a better living and gradually settled there. During the gold rush in the United States and in Australia, Chinese gold diggers went and sought their fortunes. Many of them settled in the United States. In Australia, the number of Chinese immigrants decreased dramatically after the introduction of the White Australia Policy, but still a small number settled down. Many Chinese started businesses such as laundries and restaurants and some are now working in every professional field in many countries. As most of these migrants are from southeastern China most of them speak the Cantonese dialect, Guǎngdōnghuà 廣東話, but are able to read and write Chinese characters.

The recent wave of Chinese migrants in the 20th century are people from many different social backgrounds. They are postgraduate students who study and then are employed overseas, or more recently, businessmen who are operating successful businesses, and skilled persons who specialize in a particular professional area. Most of them are from Taiwan and Hong Kong, and some are students from China. As most of these recent migrants speak Mandarin, Mandarin is becoming more and more popular in the local community and in Chinatown. However, except for the small number of people from mainland China who migrated after the reform of the Chinese language, most overseas Chinese read and write traditional characters. Local Chinese newspapers and publications are mostly printed in the traditional form. While there are a few weekend schools using simplified characters, most are still using the traditional form.

dì　bā　kè　chī　fàn
第 八 課 吃 飯

1 A note to a friend

蘭蘭：

今天上午我來找你，^{gānghǎo}剛好你出去了。你媽媽說你去^{shūdiàn}書店買書。下星期二是我的生日。我爸爸、媽媽要^{dài}帶我去中國^{fànguǎn}飯館吃飯。我想請你也一起去，時間是下午六點半，不^{zhīdào}知道你有沒有空？請你回家後打電話給我。

大偉 ^{liú}留

二〇〇二年七月十三日上午十點

2 We often go to a restaurant

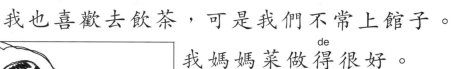

我也喜歡去飲茶，可是我們不常上館子。
我媽媽菜做^{de}得很好。

你在家^{dōu}都吃中國菜嗎？

^{píngcháng}平常都吃中國菜，
有時候也吃牛排。

^{gāitiān}改天請你到我們家吃^{biànfàn}便飯。

3 Eating at a restaurant

今天大偉、爸爸和媽媽請蘭蘭到中國飯館吃飯。

請坐，您想吃點什麼？
（zuò）

今天我點菜。請給我菜單。
（càidān）
來一盤咕咾肉，一盤麻婆豆腐，
（pán gūlǎoròu）（mápó dòufǔ）
一碗獅子頭，還有兩份春捲。
（wǎn shīzitóu）（fèn chūnjuǎn）

要喝什麼湯？
（tāng）

給我們一大碗酸辣湯。
（wǎn suānlàtāng）

4 **Eating at home**

今天蘭蘭請大偉到她家吃飯。

吃飯了。

chéng
我來盛飯。

suíbiàn zuò
大偉，來，隨便坐。

謝謝。

大偉，沒什麼菜，
zìjǐ   bié kèqì
你自己來。別客氣。

不客氣，我自己來。
āyí
阿姨菜做得真好。

你太客氣了，大偉。

níngméng-jīpiàn
真的，這檸檬雞片真好吃。

tiān   wǎn
那多吃一點。再添一碗飯吧？

bǎo
不了。我吃得太飽了。

Learn the sentences

❋ **Explaining cause**

To state a cause and its consequence, use 因為 yīnwèi......所以 suǒyǐ...... or just use 所以 suǒyǐ...... alone.

> 因為我昨天很晚回家，所以沒給你打電話。
>
> 因為他今天很晚起床(qǐchuáng)，所以遲到(chídào)了。
>
> 我快(kuài)遲到了，所以沒吃早飯。
>
> 今天的菜很好吃，所以我吃得很飽(bǎo)。
>
> 這葡萄(pútáo)太酸(suān)了，所以他不吃。

❋ **Expressing *usually* or *often***

To say that someone usually does something, use 平常 píngcháng. For example, to say I usually get up early, say 我平常都很早起床。Wǒ píngcháng dōu hěn zǎo qǐchuáng. To say that someone does something often, use 常常 chángcháng or 常 cháng and to say not often, use 不常 bù cháng. For example, to say I often go swimming, say 我常去游泳。Wǒ cháng qù yóuyǒng; to say I don't go swimming often, say 我不常去游泳。Wǒ bù cháng qù yóuyǒng.

平常 usually	我們平常都吃中國菜。
	我平常都很早起床。
常常；常 often	我們常常上館子。
	我星期天常去游泳。
不常 not often	我不常上館子。
	我不常去百貨(bǎihuò)公司(gōngsī)。

✳ **Offering a choice**

When offering a choice, use 還是 háishì which means or. To ask Do you want to have steamed rice or fried rice? say 你要吃白飯還是炒飯。Nǐ yào chī báifàn háishì chǎofàn?

你要吃白飯還是炒飯?	炒飯。
你要買襯衫^{chènshān}還是T恤^{xù}?	我要買襯衫。
你要紅色的還是白色的?	我要白色的。
你要去打籃球^{lánqiú}還是去游泳?	去打籃球。
他在看漫畫^{mànhuà}還是在做功課^{gōngkè}?	看漫畫。
你喜歡游泳還是打球?	我喜歡打球。
這條裙子太寬^{tiáo qúnzi kuān}還是太窄^{zhǎi}?	太窄了。

New words and expressions

剛好	gānghǎo	just, happen to
出去	chūqù	to go out chū- to go out; qù- to go
帶……去	dài...qù	to take... to dài- to take, to bring; qù- to go
飯館	fànguǎn	restaurant, or said 餐館 cānguǎn
後	hòu	after; back, behind
留	liú	to leave (a note)
因為	yīnwèi	because yīn- cause; wèi- for
回家	huíjiā	to go home huí- to return; jiā- home
所以	suǒyǐ	therefore suǒ- so; yǐ- to use
邀請	yāoqǐng	invitation; to invite
常常	chángcháng	often
館子	guǎnzi	restaurant, used more often in southern China, going to a restaurant – 上館子 shàng guǎnzi
尤其	yóuqí	especially

飲茶	yǐnchá	to have dimsum, a Cantonese meal of small snacks and tea
		yǐn- to drink; chá- tea
平常	píngcháng	usually píng- smooth; cháng- often, usually
有時候	yǒushíhòu	sometimes
牛排	niúpái	steak niú- cow, bull; pái(gǔ)- spareribs
改天	gǎitiān	some other day gǎi- to change; tiān- day
便飯	biànfàn	[modest form] a simple meal biàn- convenient
點菜	diǎncài	to order food diǎn- to choose, hour; cài- dish, vegetable
菜單	càidān	menu cài- dish, vegetable; dān- list
來……	lái...	give (us/me) ... (used when ordering food)
盤	pán	[a measure word for dish] plate
麻婆豆腐	mápó-dòufǔ	name of a hot and spicy bean curd dish, said to be named
		after a woman who was skilled in cooking this dish
		mápó- old woman with a pockmarked face; dòufǔ- bean curd
碗	wǎn	[a measure word for rice or soup] bowl
獅子頭	shīzitóu	name of a dish of fried meatballs shīzi- lion; tóu- head
湯	tāng	soup
酸辣湯	suānlàtāng	hot and sour soup suān- sour; là- hot
白飯	báifàn	plain rice, called 米飯 mǐfàn in China
		mǐ- uncooked rice
還是	háishì	or
對了	duìle	by the way
放	fàng	to put; to let off, to let go
味精	wèijīng	monosodium glutamate (M.S.G.)
客人	kèrén	guest kè- guest; rén- person
多	duō	more, a lot
結帳	jiézhàng	to settle an account
盛飯	chéng fàn	to serve rice, to fill a bowl with rice
隨便坐	suíbiàn zuò	sit anywhere suíbiàn- to do as one pleases; zuò- to sit
自己來	zìjǐ lái	to help oneself zìjǐ- self; lái- to help, do, come
別客氣	bié kèqì	don't stand on ceremony; don't be formal;
		make yourself at home kèqì- courteous
不客氣	bú kèqì	not being courteous; not at all; you are welcome
添	tiān	to add
飽	bǎo	to be full

Write the characters

因	為	所	常	館
yīn *cause, reason*	wèi *for*	suǒ *so; place*	cháng *often*	guǎn *shop, building*
子	飲	茶	都	平
zi *[suffix]*	yǐn *to drink*	chá *tea*	dōu *all*	píng *smooth*
客	氣	湯	炒	得
kè *guest*	qì *manner; air*	tāng *soup*	chǎo *to stir-fry*	de *[degree, result of]*

做 得 很 好

林朋喜歡吃炒飯，可是學校不賣炒飯。他
在學校平常都吃三明治(sānmíngzhì)、漢堡(hànbǎo)和熱狗(règǒu)。上星期四
中午吃飯時，林朋說他很想吃炒飯。王利說他會
做炒飯，他可以早上在家裡做，中
午請林朋吃。

星期五早上，因為王利很晚
起床(qǐchuáng)，所以他去學校旁邊(pángbiān)的中國
館子買了炒飯，中午請林朋吃。
現在林朋常常說：「王利炒飯做得
很好。」

在 此 小 便

A man urinated at a street corner where the sign 行人等不得在此小便 could be clearly seen. This sign is read as「行人等，不得在此小便。Xíngrén děng, bù dé zài cǐ xiǎobiàn.」It means *Pedestrians etc. cannot urinate here*.

He was caught by a policeman. The policeman asked him: "Didn't you see the sign there?" The man answered: "Yes. That's why I did it. You see, it says 行人，等不得，在此小便。Xíngrén, děng bù dé, zài cǐ xiǎobiàn." The way this man read the sign change the meaning into *Pedestrians who cannot wait urinate here*.

From this sign we can see that some words have different meanings from what we have learned. On the sign, 行人 xíngrén means *pedestrians*; 等 děng means *et cetera*; 不得 bù dé means *cannot*; 此 cǐ means *here*; and 小便 xiǎobiàn means *urine or to urinate*. When the man read the sign he used 等 děng meaning *wait* instead of meaning *et cetera*.

Now we have learned that 小便 xiǎobiàn means *urine or to urinate*. Can you work out what 大便 dàbiàn means?

Something to know

❀ Food balance

Chinese believe that food contains the nature of yīn 陰 or yáng 陽, that is, having *the properties of cooling or warming*. Cooling foods such as bean curd, watermelon, celery and green tea often contain less calories while warming foods such as cherries, ginger, chilli, meat and black tea often contain more calories. Cooking methods can alter the cooling or warming nature of food. For example, deep-fried foods tend to be warming and pickled foods are cooling. A balance of cooling and warming foods is important in the Chinese diet.

❀ Bean curd in Chinese diet

Bean curd, dòufǔ 豆腐, which is made from soybeans and is high in protein, is a favorite of most Chinese. Not having much flavor in itself, dòufǔ combines well with almost any ingredients to produce a great variety of tastes. It can be steamed, boiled, deep-fried, or shallow-fried. Dòfǔ is used in simple cooking for the family daily meal while it can also be a luxurious dish for a special occasion. The popular hot and spicy dish mápó dòufǔ 麻婆豆腐 is said to have been invented by a pockmarked-faced widow who ran a little restaurant for a living. The term mápó means *pockmarked-faced old woman*.

✿ Family meal

The family meal is generally simpler than that at a restaurant. The staple food is rice in southern China and wheat products in northern China. Although meals vary from place to place and from day to day, a typical breakfast may consist of rice porridge with eggs and pickled vegetables, or soybean milk with sesame seed cakes, shāobǐng 燒餅, and deep-fried dough sticks, yóutiáo 油條. For lunch, it could be a bowl of noodle soup and for dinner, rice or steamed buns with vegetables, soup and meat or fish.

The Chinese habitually have their rice and other dishes first and the soup last. However, most Chinese restaurants overseas have adopted the Western style and serve the soup at the beginning of the meal.

When guests are invited for a meal at home, the Chinese often use modest words at the table. Wǒ tàitai bú huì zuò cài 我太太不會做菜, Cài zuò de bù hǎo 菜做得不好, or Méi shéme cài 沒什麼菜, are commonly used although there may be a full table of their best cooking.

✿ Formal feast

A formal Chinese feast commonly consists of 10 to 12 courses, starting with a cold dish and ending with a sweet dish. The seating arrangement is regarded as important at a formal feast, although it is not normally practiced for a daily meal at home. At a round table, the seat facing the door is for the guest of honor and the seat with the back to the door is the host's. Couples normally sit together. This arrangement and the short distance over the round table facilitates conversation between the guest and the host.

沒什麼菜, 請自己來。

Seat of host

Seats of hosts

Formal table seating

dì　jiǔ　kè　tiānqì
第 九 課 天 氣

1 What's the weather today? 今天天氣怎麼樣？

xiàyǔ
今天下雨。

xiàxuě
今天下雪。

guā　fēng
今天刮大風。

今天天氣很好。

rè
今天很熱。

lěng
今天很冷。

liángkuài
今天很涼快。

2 Taipei's weather

一年有四季。每^{jì}季有三個月。

台^{Táiběi}北的春^{chūntiān}天是三月到五月；夏^{xiàtiān}天是六月到八月；
秋^{qiūtiān}天是九月到十一月；冬^{dōngtiān}天是十二月到二月。

台北的春天很暖^{nuǎnhuō}和，但^{dànshì}是常常下雨。

　　冬天不下雪，但是寒^{hánliú}流來時風又大、又冷。

台北的夏天很悶^{mēnrè}熱，常常令^{lìng}人汗^{hànliú-jiábèi}流浹背。

　　秋天天^{tiānkōng}空晴^{qínglǎng}朗，令人覺^{juéde}得身^{shēnxīn-shūchàng}心舒暢。

3 Weather report

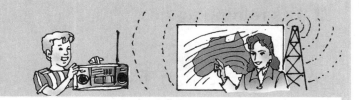

昨天的天氣：
陰（yīn），午後有雨。
最高氣溫華氏八十四度（zuìgāo qìwēn huáshì ... dù），
最低七十五度（zuìdī）。

今天的天氣預報（yùbào）：
上午晴（qíng），下午有雷陣雨（léizhènyǔ）。
最高氣溫華氏八十九度，
最低七十七度。

明天的天氣預報：
晴，有時多雲（duōyún）。
最高氣溫華氏九十三度，
最低八十二度。

(Handwritten notes in top margin)
what about Xiao Ming know, and why not?
Is it going to be cold, and where are the boys going?
Why is Xiao Ming going back to sleep
How do you say "I slept like a log"?

4 It's raining again

昨天晚上又下雨了。 (yòu)

真的啊！我一點都不知道。 (a) (zhīdào)
我大概睡得太死了。現在還下雨嗎？ (dàgài) (shuì) (sǐ)

現在雨停了。 (tíng)
今天我想去游泳。你去不去？

不去。我還想睡覺。 (shuìjiào)

天氣預報説今天會很熱。 (yùbào)

多熱？最高氣溫幾度？ (qìwēn)

九十八度。起床！去游泳吧！ (qǐchuáng)

好吧！

(After breakfast) 真討厭！又下雨了。 (tǎoyàn)

太好了。下雨天是睡覺天，我再去睡覺。 (shuìjiào)

 **Learn the sentences**

✳ **Inquiring about the weather**

To ask What's the weather like today? say 今天天氣怎麼樣？ Jīntiān tiānqì zěmeyàng? To answer, state the condition, such as It's raining today. say 今天下雨。Jīntiān xiàyǔ; and It is cold today. say 今天很冷。Jīntiān hěn lěng.

今天天氣怎麼樣？	今天下雨。
	今天很冷。
昨天天氣怎麼樣？	昨天刮大風。
	昨天天氣很好，很涼快。
明天天氣怎麼樣？	明天會下雪。
	明天會很熱。

✳ **Use of 會 huì to indicate the future**

The word 會 huì is often used to describe something which is going to or likely to happen in the future. For example, to say It's going to rain tomorrow., say 明天會下雨。Míngtiān huì xiàyǔ.

明天天氣怎麼樣？	明天會下雨。
	天氣預報說明天會很冷。
你看明天會下雨嗎？	大概不會吧！
蘭蘭下午會回來嗎？	會，她下午三點回來。
林老師明天會走嗎？	他明天不會走。

✳ **Use of 到 dào to indicate length of time**

The word 到 dào is used to indicate a duration of time and is equivalent to the English word to. To say January to February, say 一月到二月 yī yuè dào èr yuè .

北京的春天：	三月到五月
澳洲的春天： Àozhōu	九月到十一月
上學的時間：	上午九點到下午三點
看電視的時間： diànshì	晚上七點到七點半
做功課的時間： gōngkè	晚上七點半到九點半

✳ **Use of 死 sǐ to describe an extreme condition**

The word 死 sǐ, which literally means to die or dead, can also be used in conversation as a stative verb to describe an extreme condition. Therefore, to express I'm starving (extremely hungry), say 我餓死了。Wǒ è sǐ le.

我睡得太死了。
shuì　　sǐ

我餓死了！我們去吃點東西吧！
dōngxī

今天熱死了。

【小笑話】
xiàohuà

　　老林在小王家做客。因為下雨，老林住了很多天還
Lín　　Wáng
不走，所以小王寫了一首詩：「下雨天留客天留我不留」
　　shǒu shī　　　　　liú
他的意思是：「下雨天留客，天留，我不留。」老林看
yìsi
到這首詩，他念：「下雨天，留客天，留我不？留。」
niàn
他很高興，又多住了幾天。
gāoxìng

New words and expressions

天氣	tiānqì	weather tiān- sky, day; qì- air
下雨	xiàyǔ	to rain xià- (of rain or snow) to fall, under; yǔ- rain
下雪	xiàxuě	to snow xià- (of rain or snow) to fall, under; xuě- snow
刮風	guāfēng	windy (extremely windy – 刮大風 guā dà fēng) guā- to blow; fēng- wind
熱	rè	hot
冷	lěng	cold
涼快	liángkuài	cool and pleasant liáng- cool; kuài- happy, fast
季	jì	season
每	měi	every
台北	Táiběi	the capital city of R.O.C. tái- platform; běi- north
春天	chūntiān	spring chūn- spring; tiān- sky, day
到	dào	to, until; to reach
夏天	xiàtiān	summer xià- summer; tiān- sky, day
秋天	qiūtiān	autumn qiū- autumn; tiān- sky, day
冬天	dōngtiān	winter dōng- winter; tiān- sky, day
暖和	nuǎnhuō	warm
但是	dànshì	but, however
寒流	hánliú	a cold current, polar current hán- cold; liú- current, to flow
悶熱	mēnrè	sultry mēn- suffocating; rè- hot
令人	lìngrén	make people..., let people...
汗流浹背	hànliú-jiábèi	streaming with sweat hàn- sweat; liú- flow; jiá- totally wet; bèi- back
天空	tiānkōng	sky tiān- sky; kōng- empty
晴朗	qínglǎng	sunny, fine and cloudless qíng- fine; lǎng- clear (weather)
覺得	juéde	to feel
身心舒暢	shēnxīn- shūchàng	pleasant physically and mentally shēn- body; xīn- mind shū- comfortable; chàng- free
陰	yīn	cloudy (cloudy day – 陰天 yīntiān)
午後	wǔhòu	afternoon wǔ- noon; hòu- after
最高	zuìgāo	highest zuì- the most; gāo- high
氣溫	qìwēn	temperature qì- air; wēn- temperature, warm
華氏	huáshì	Fahrenheit (centigrade– 攝氏 shèshì)
度	dù	degree
最低	zuìdī	lowest zuì- the most; dī- low

預報	yùbào	forecast yù- in advance; bào- report
晴	qíng	fine; fine day – 晴天 qíngtiān
雷陣雨	léizhènyǔ	thunder shower léi- thunder; zhènyǔ- shower
有時	yǒushí	sometimes
多雲	duōyún	cloudy duō- a lot, more; yún- cloud
又	yòu	again
死	sǐ	deathly; dead; to die
停	tíng	to stop
多熱	duó rè	How hot?
討厭	tǎoyàn	annoying; to hate tǎo- to incur; yàn- to be disgusted with
北京	Běijīng	the capital city of China běi- north; jīng- capital
老林	Lǎo Lín	Old Lin
小王	Xiǎo Wáng	Little Wang
做客	zuòkè	to be a guest zuò- to be, to do; kè- guest
首	shǒu	[a measure word for poem]
詩	shī	poem
意思	yìsi	meaning
念	niàn	to read
高興	gāoxìng	happy gāo- high; xìng- excitement
幾天	jǐtiān	a few days jǐ- an uncertain number, how many; tiān- day

春

夏

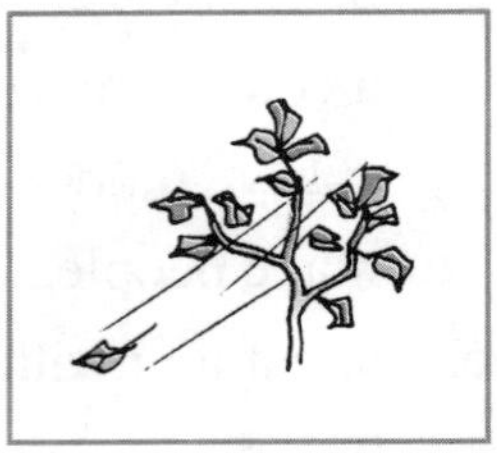

秋

冬

冷

熱

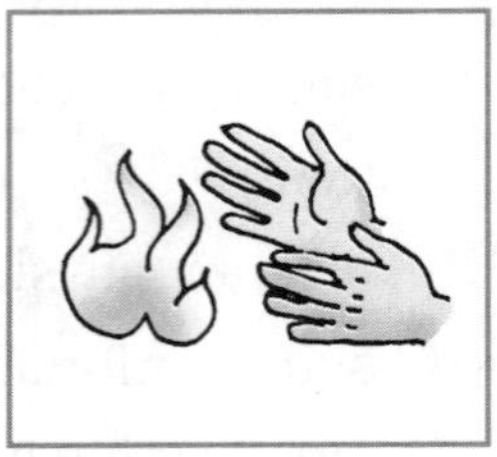

暖

涼

晴天

陰天

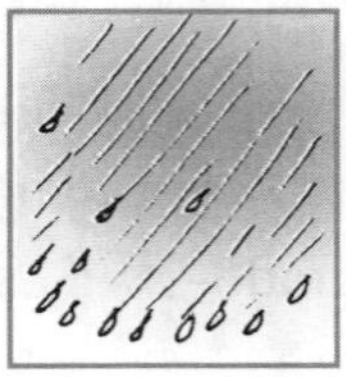

雨天

刮風

下雨

下雪

Write the characters

雨 yǔ *rain*	雪 xuě *snow*	刮 guā *to blow (wind)*	風 fēng *wind*	熱 rè *hot*
冷 lěng *cold*	涼 liáng *cool*	春 chūn *spring*	夏 xià *summer*	秋 qiū *autumn, fall*
冬 dōng *winter*	台 tái *platform, Taiwan*	北 běi *north*	暖 nuǎn *warm*	陰 yīn *cloudy*
晴 qíng *sunny*	最 zuì *the most*	高 gāo *high*	低 dī *low*	度 dù *degree*

bié
別 去 了

　　早上林朋到王利家，他們要一起去打
網球。今天天氣很熱，林朋到的時候气温是
（wǎngqiú）　　　　　　　　　　　　　（qìwēn）
華氏一百度。王利説：「這麼熱，別去打網球
（huáshì）　　　　　　　　　　（bié）
了。我看，我們上午在家看電視，下午去
　　　　　　　　　　　　　　（diànshì）
游泳。」吃午飯的時候，電視的天氣預報説，
　　　　　　　　　　　　　　　　（yùbào）
下午有雷陣雨，會刮大風和下大雨。王利説：
（léizhènyǔ）　　（guā）
「我看，別去游泳了。我們看錄影帶吧！」
　　　　　　　　　　　（lùyǐngdài）

Something to know

❀ Climate in China

Due to the vastness of the country, the weather in China varies dramatically from region to region. The country covers a total area of approximately 3.7 million square miles with mountains in the west and plains in the east. The climate ranges from frigid in the north to tropical in the south. The average annual rainfall is 1,500 mm in the humid southeast and only 50 mm in the arid northwest. The hottest area in summer is in Turpan, Tǔlǔfān 吐魯番, in Xīnjiāng 新疆 where the average daytime temperature in July exceeds 104°F. The coldest area is in the Hǎilār 海拉爾 district in Inner Mongolia, Nèi Ménggǔ 內蒙古, where the average temperature in January is -17.8°F. Hēilóngjiāng 黑龍江 province is entirely without summer, and Hǎinán Island 海南島 is virtually without winter. In the Huáihé 淮河 basin, the four seasons are clearly defined, while in Kūnmíng 昆明, it is springlike all year round.

❀ Key tourist spots in China

With a vast land and a long history, China has plentiful physical and cultural attractions. Tourists are fascinated by the beautiful scenery of the ancient sacred mountains: Tàishān 泰山 in Shāndōng 山東 province and Huáshān 華山 in Shǎnxī 陝西 province. Visitors to Tàishān can climb up 7,000 steps to its peak to admire the beauty of nature. West Lake, Xīhú 西湖, in Hángzhōu 杭州 was a favorite topic for ancient poets and still displays poetic beauty. The limestone pinnacles in Guìlín 桂林 and the Stone Forest, Shílín 石林, in Yúnnán 雲南 province, exhibit the fantastic craft of nature.

The Buddhist murals and statues in the caves of Dūnhuáng 敦煌 and Yúngāng 雲岡, and the giant 230-foot high Buddha at the hill of Lèshān 樂山 are masterpieces of human endeavor. The unearthed terracotta warriors in Xī'ān 西安 are representative of the empire of Qín Shǐhuáng 秦始皇.

A scene of the limestone pinnacles along the Li River in Guìlín 桂林

The giant Buddha in Lèshān 樂山

Chángchéng 長城, the Great Wall

In Běijīng 北京, the renovated section of the Great Wall, Chángchéng 長城, in Bādálǐng 八達嶺 tells of the history of Chinese expansion. The Forbidden City, Zǐjìnchéng 紫禁城, presents the magnificence of the ancient palace, and Fragrance Hill, Xiāngshān 香山, displays its splendid red foliage in fall.

❀ Key tourist spots in Taiwan

An island only slightly larger than Massachusetts and Connecticut combined, with its highest mountain at 12,000 feet, provides Taiwan with spectacular scenery. Taroko Gorge, Tàilǔgé 太魯閣, at the entrance of the Cross-island Highway, Héngguàn Gōnglù 橫貫公路, features a magnificent marble gorge; Ali mountain, Ālǐshān 阿里山, displays a turbulent sea of clouds and a beautiful sunrise; The National Chungshan Museum, Zhōngshān Bówùyuàn 中山博物院 (or briefly called Gùgōng 故宮) shows the abundant treasures of Chinese culture.

Zhōngshān Bówùyuàn 中山博物院 in Taipei, Taiwan

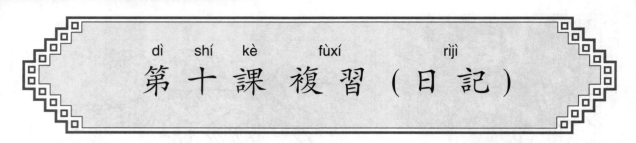

1 A diary

二○○二年十二月七日，星期六，晴

今天是星期六，天氣很好。上午很涼快，可

是下午非常熱。

我今天很早起床。上午我和媽媽去百貨公司

買東西。媽媽的皮鞋壞了，她買了一雙黑色的

皮鞋。我的褲子破了，我買了一條白色的褲子。

中午我們到中國館子飲茶。我們一家人常常上館

子吃中國菜，我尤其喜歡去飲茶。

今天是美怡的生日。下午三點，蘭蘭和我請

她看電影。美怡今天穿一件淺黃色的洋裝，看起

來很漂亮；蘭蘭穿紅襯衫、黑裙子，非常時髦。

明天早上六點我和爸爸去釣魚。今天晚上要

早點睡覺。

2 Language Functions

[1]　Asking the date

今天是幾月幾號？ Jīntiān shì jǐ yuè jǐ hào?

今天是三月八號。Jīntiān shì sān yuè bā hào.

Asking the day of the week

今天是星期幾？ Jīntiān shì xīngqí jǐ?

今天是星期三。Jīntiān shì xīngqísān.

Asking the year someone was born

你是哪年生的？ Nǐ shì nǎ nián shēng de?

我是一九六九年生的。Wǒ shì yī jiǔ liù jiǔ nián shēng de.

Seeking permission

我明天去看電影，可以嗎？ Wǒ míngtiān qù kàn diànyǐng, kěyǐ ma?

可以。Kěyǐ.　or　不行。Bù xíng.

Asking about birthdays

你的生日是什麼時候？ Nǐ de shēngrì shì shéme shíhòu?

我的生日是七月十四號。Wǒ de shēngrì shì qī yuè shísì hào.

Stating the date

今天是二〇〇二年十二月四日，星期三。

Jīntiān shì èr líng líng èr nián shí'èr yuè sì rì, xīngqísān.

[2]　Finding out what someone is doing

你在做什麼？ Nǐ zài zuò shéme?

我在做功課。Wǒ zài zuò gōngkè.

Asking the time

現在幾點？ Xiànzài jǐ diǎn?

現在七點十五分。Xiànzài qī diǎn shíwǔ fēn.

Asking what time someone does something

你幾點上學？ Nǐ jǐ diǎn shàngxué?

我八點半上學。Wǒ bā diǎn bàn shàngxué.

Use of "了 le"

好了！好了！ Hǎo le! Hǎo le!

太好了！ Tài hǎo le!

我的書包壞了。Wǒ de shūbāo huài le.

你遲到了。Nǐ chídào le.

他來了。Tā lái le.

[3]　Asking the location of something

請問，廁所（洗手間）在哪裡？ Qǐngwèn, cèsuǒ (xǐshǒujiān) zài nǎlǐ?

在最後面。Zài zuì hòumiàn.

Asking what someone is doing somewhere

他在客廳做什麼？ Tā zài kètīng zuò shéme?

看電視。Kàn diànshì.

Asking where someone is doing something

他在哪裡做功課？ Tā zài nǎlǐ zuò gōngkè?

在電視機前面！ Zài diànshìjī qiánmiàn!

Asking what happened

怎麼回事？ Zěme huí shì?

他的褲子破了。 Tā de kùzi pò le.

Finding out where someone sleeps

你昨天晚上睡哪裡？ Nǐ zuótiān wǎnshang shuì nǎlǐ?

睡客廳沙發。 Shuì kètīng shāfā.

[4] **Asking what someone is wearing**

她今天穿什麼衣服？ Tā jīntiān chuān shéme yīfú?

她穿黃色的洋裝。 Tā chuān huángsè de yángzhuāng.

Describing how clothes fit

這雙皮鞋太小了。 Zhè shuāng píxié tài xiǎo le.

這件旗袍很合身。 Zhè jiàn qípáo hěn héshēn.

Use of "起來 qǐlai" after the verb

這雙功夫鞋穿起來很舒服。 Zhè shuāng gōngfū xié chuān qǐlái hěn shūfú.

這條裙子看起來很漂亮。 Zhè tiáo qúnzi kàn qǐlái hěn piàoliàng.

Wondering what to wear

我明天該穿什麼衣服呢？ Wǒ míngtiān gāi chuān shéme yīfú ne?

你該穿西裝。 Nǐ gāi chuān xīzhuāng.

Asking for an opinion

你看這件怎麼樣？ Nǐ kàn zhè jiàn chènshān zěmeyàng?

挺好看的。 Tǐng hǎokàn de.

Use of "有沒有 yǒu méi yǒu" for a past event

你今天有沒有吃早飯？ Nǐ jīntiān yǒu méi yǒu chī zǎofàn?

有，我吃了。 Yǒu, wǒ chī le. or 我沒吃。 Wǒ méi chī.

[5] **Asking the price**

這本書多少錢？ Zhè běn shū duōshǎo qián? 三塊半。 Sān kuài bàn.

蘋果怎麼賣？ Píngguǒ zěme mài? 一斤一塊四。 Yì jīn yí kuài sì.

Asking if something is for sale

你們賣字典嗎？ Nǐmen mài zìdiǎn ma?

賣。 Mài. or 不賣。 Bú mài.

你們有沒有字典？ Nǐmen yǒu méi yǒu zìdiǎn?

有。 Yǒu. or 沒有。 Méi yǒu.

Expressing an opinion on goods or asking for a choice

這個挺好的，可是太貴。 Zhè ge tǐng hǎo de, kěshì tài guì le.

這件襯衫太大了，有沒有小一點的？

Zhè jiàn chènshān tài dà le, yǒu méi yǒu xiǎo yìdiǎn de?

Asking whether something is sweet or sour

葡萄甜不甜（酸不酸）？ Pútáo tián bù tián (suān bù suān)?

很甜。 Hěn tián. or 不酸。 Bù suān.

[6] **Asking if someone is available**

你明天有空嗎？ Nǐ míngtiān yǒu kòng ma?

有。 Yǒu. or 沒有。 Méi yǒu.

Asking where someone lives

你住在哪裡？ Nǐ zhù zài nǎlǐ? 我住在舊金山。 Wǒ zhù zài Jiùjīnshān.

Asking someone's telephone number

你家的電話是幾號？ Nǐ jiā de diànhuà shì jǐ hào?

九八七六五四三。 Jiǔ bā qī liù wǔ sì sān.

Asking if someone is home

請問他在家嗎？ Qǐngwèn tā zài jiā ma?

在。Zài.　　or　　不在。Bú zài.

Use of "一下 yíxià"

請你等一下，他馬上來。 Qǐng nǐ děng yíxià, tā mǎshàng lái.

來，我給你們介紹一下。 Lái, wǒ gěi nǐmen jièshào yíxià.

[7] Asking who is speaking on the phone

您是哪位？ Nín shì nǎ /něi wèi?

我是大偉的同學。 Wǒ shì Dàwěi de tóngxué.

Asking someone who he/she is looking for

你找誰？ Nǐ zhǎo shéi?

我找李老師。 Wǒ zhǎo Lǐ lǎoshī.

Asking to talk to someone on the phone

我找林老師，請問他在家嗎？ Wǒ zhǎo Lín lǎoshī, qǐngwèn tā zài jiā ma?

我就是。Wǒ jiù shì.　　or　　在。Zài.　　or　　不在。Bú zài.

Asking if someone has come back

請問蘭蘭回來了嗎？ Qǐngwèn Lánlán huílái le ma?

回來了。Huílái le.　　or　　還沒回來。Hái méi huílái.

Asking when someone is coming back

他幾點回來？ Tā jǐ diǎn huílái?

下午四點半。Xiàwǔ sì diǎn bàn.

Asking someone the purpose of going somewhere

你去他家做什麼？ Nǐ qù tā jiā zuò shéme?　　去玩。Qù wán.

[8] Explaining cause

因為我太晚起床，所以沒吃早飯。

Yīnwèi wǒ tài wǎn qǐchuáng, suǒyǐ méi chī zǎofàn.

Offering a choice

你要去游泳還是打球？ Nǐ yào qù yóuyǒng háishì dǎqiú?

我要去游泳。Wǒ yào qù yóuyǒng.　　or　　我要去打球。Wǒ yào qù dǎqiú.

[9] Inquiring about the weather

今天天氣怎麼樣？ Jīntiān tiānqì zěmeyàng?

今天很熱。Jīntiān hěn rè.

明天會下雨嗎？ Míngtiān huì xiàyǔ ma?

會。Huì.　　or　　不會。Bú huì.

Stating the length of time

台北的春天：三月到五月。Táiběi de chūntiān: sān yuè dào wǔ yuè.

吃飯的時間：下午十二點半到一點半。

Chī wǔfàn de shíjiān: xiàwǔ shí'èr diǎn bàn dào yì diǎn bàn.

Use "死 sǐ" to describe an extreme condition

我餓死了。Wǒ è sǐ le.

今天熱死了。Jīntiān rè sǐ le.

Appendix 1

WORDS AND EXPRESSIONS
Chinese-English

m.w.- measure word

Traditonal	Pinyin	English	Simplified	Lesson
A 阿姨	āyí	[*address*] woman of one's mother's age; (in Taiwan) mother's sister	阿姨	6
唉	ài	(a sigh)	唉	3
B 白	bái	white	白	4
白飯	báifàn	(in Taiwan) plain rice	白饭	8
白宮	Báigōng	White House	白宫	6
白色	báisè	white	白色	4
百貨公司	bǎihuò gōngsī	department store	百货公司	5
拜訪	bàifǎng	to visit	拜访	6
半	bàn	half	半	2
半夜	bànyè	midnight	半夜	3
飽	bǎo	to be full	饱	8
報紙	bàozhǐ	newspaper	报纸	5
北京	Běijīng	the capital city of China	北京	9
本	běn	[*m.w.* - book, magazine etc.]	本	5
便飯	biànfàn	[modest form] a simple meal	便饭	8
錶	biǎo	watch	表	2
別客氣	bié kèqì	don't be formal; make yourself at home	别客气	8
冰箱	bīngxiāng	refrigerator	冰箱	4
菠蘿	bōluó	pineapple (used in China), also called 鳳梨 fènglí	菠萝	5
不客氣	bú kèqì	not being courteous; not at all; you are welcome	不客气	8
不用	búyòng	need not	不用	6
C 猜	cāi	to guess	猜	3
菜單	càidān	menu	菜单	8
草莓	cǎoméi	strawberry	草莓	5
廁所	cèsuǒ	restroom, lavatory	厕所	3
差	chā	differ from	差	2
長	cháng	long	长	4
常	cháng	often	常	6
常常	chángcháng	often	常常	8
唱歌	chànggē	to sing	唱歌	3
車	chē	car, vehicle	车	3
車庫	chēkù	garage	车库	3
車子	chēzi	car, small vehicle	车子	3
襯衫	chènshān	shirt	衬衫	4

Traditonal	Pinyin	English	Simplified	Lesson
盛飯	chéng fàn	to serve rice, to fill a bowl with rice	盛饭	8
橙色	chéngsè	orange (color)	橙色	4
遲到	chídào	to arrive late	迟到	2
出來	chūlái	to come out	出来	6
出口	chūkǒu	exit	出口	7
出去	chūqù	to go out	出去	8
廚房	chúfáng	kitchen	厨房	3
穿	chuān	to wear (clothes, shoes or socks)	穿	4
穿起來	chuān qǐlái	impression or feeling of the clothes on someone	穿起来	4
串	chuàn	[m.w. - bananas, grapes] bunch, cluster	串	5
春天	chūntiān	spring	春天	9
錯	cuò	wrong, incorrect	错	1

D 打	dǎ	to play (ball game, taichi etc.);	打	3
		to dial (telephone)		3
打擾	dǎrǎo	to disturb, to trouble	打扰	6
大便	dàbiàn	excrement; to empty the bowels	大便	8
大概	dàgài	probably	大概	1
大人	dàrén	adults	大人	3
大學	dàxué	university	大学	6
袋	dài	bag	袋	5
帶……去	dài...qù	to take ... to	带……去	8
蛋糕	dàngāo	cake	蛋糕	1
但是	dànshì	but; however	但是	9
倒霉	dǎoméi	to have bad luck	倒霉	3
到	dào	to go to, to arrive;	到	5
		to, until		9
等	děng	to wait	等	6
等一下	děng yíxià	to wait a moment	等一下	6
低	dī	low	低	9
地板	dìbǎn	floor	地板	3
地圖	dìtú	map	地图	5
點	diǎn	o'clock; dot;	点	2
		a little		5
		to choose (food)		8
點菜	diǎncài	to order food	点菜	8
電冰箱	diànbīngxiāng	refrigerator	电冰箱	3
電話	diànhuà	telephone	电话	3
電視	diànshì	television	电视	3
電視機	diànshìjī	television set	电视机	3
電影	diànyǐng	movie	电影	2
釣魚	diàoyú	to fish	钓鱼	1
頂	dǐng	[m.w. - hat, cap]	顶	5
冬天	dōngtiān	winter	冬天	9
都	dōu	already; all	都	3
度	dù	degree (temperature)	度	9

Traditonal	Pinyin	English	Simplified	Lesson
短	duǎn	short (length)	短	4
短褲	duǎnkù	shorts	短裤	4
對	duì	right, correct	对	1
對了	duìle	by the way	对了	8
對面	duìmiàn	opposite (location)	对面	3
多	duō	more, a lot; how	多	8
多熱	duó rè	how hot	多热	9
多少	duōshǎo	how much, how many	多少	5
多雲	duōyún	cloudy	多云	9

F 飯館	fànguǎn	restaurant	饭馆	8
飯廳	fàntīng	dining room	饭厅	3
房子	fángzi	house	房子	3
放	fàng	to let off, to let go, to release;	放	2
		to put		8
放學	fàngxué	to finish classes (classes are over)	放学	2
非常	fēicháng	extremely	非常	5
肥	féi	loose-fitting (clothing), used in China; fat	肥	4
分	fēn	minute;	分	2
		one-cent unit = 0.01 块 kuài or 元 yuán		5
份	fèn	[m.w. - newspaper, copy etc.]	份	5
風	fēng	wind, breeze	风	9
風箏	fēngzhēng	kite	风筝	2
鳳梨	fènglí	pineapple, called 菠蘿 bōluó in China	凤梨	5
父親	fùqīn	father	父亲	6

G 該	gāi	should	该	2
改天	gǎitiān	some other day	改天	8
剛好	gānghǎo	just, happen to	刚好	8
高	gāo	high, tall	高	9
高興	gāoxìng	happy	高兴	9
給	gěi	to give	给	5
功夫鞋	gōngfū xié	Chinese soft shoes originally the footwear of martial arts	功夫鞋	7
功課	gōngkè	homework, school work	功课	2
公寓	gōngyù	apartments	公寓	3
工作	gōngzuò	work; to work	工作	6
咕嚕肉	gūlūròu	sweet and sour pork	咕噜肉	8
咕咾肉	gūlǎoròu	sweet and sour pork	古老肉	8
刮風	guāfēng	windy	刮风	9
館子	guǎnzi	restaurant	馆子	8
貴	guì	expensive	贵	5
過癮	guòyǐn	to one's heart's content, fully enjoyed	过瘾	6

H 還	hái	also; still	还	3
還不錯	hái búcuò	[oral] not bad, pretty good	还不错	5

Traditonal	Pinyin	English	Simplified	Lesson
還是	háishì	or	还是	8
寒流	hánliú	cold current	寒流	9
汗流浹背	hànliú-jiábèi	streaming with sweat	汗流浃背	9
漢英字典	Hàn-Yīng zìdiǎn	Chinese-English dictionary	汉英字典	5
好了好了	hǎo le hǎo le	that's enough	好了好了	1
好看	hǎokàn	good-looking	好看	4
好像	hǎoxiàng	seem, be like	好像	4
號	hào	date; number	号	1
號碼	hàomǎ	number	号码	8
喝茶	hē chá	to have tea	喝茶	2
合身	héshēn	well-fitting (clothing)	合身	4
黑色	hēisè	black	黑色	4
紅	hóng	red	红	4
後	hòu	after; back, behind	后	8
後面	hòumiàn	behind	后面	3
後年	hòunián	the year after next	后年	1
後天	hòutiān	the day after tomorrow	后天	1
花園	huāyuán	garden	花园	3
華氏	huáshì	Fahrenheit	华氏	9
壞	huài	broken down; bad	坏	3
皇后	huánghòu	queen	皇后	6
黃色	huángsè	yellow	黄色	4
回答	huídá	to answer	回答	6
回家	huíjiā	to go home	回家	8
回來	huílái	to come back, to return	回来	3
會	huì	will; can, be able to	会	6

J

幾點鐘	jǐ diǎn zhōng	what time	几点钟	7
幾天	jǐtiān	a few days	几天	9
季	jì	season	季	9
間	jiān	[m.w. - room]; within (time, space)	间	3, 6
見	jiàn	to see, to catch sight of	见	3
件	jiàn	[m.w. - clothing or affair]	件	4
教書	jiāoshū	to teach (at school)	教书	6
角	jiǎo	[formal] 10-cent unit	角	5
街	jiē	street	街	6
接	jiē	to meet, to pick (someone) up	接	7
結帳	jiézhàng	to settle an account	结帐	8
介紹	jièshào	to introduce	介绍	6
斤	jīn	a unit of weight = 0.6 kg in Taiwan = 0.5 kg in China	斤	5
今年	jīnnián	this year	今年	1
今天	jīntiān	today	今天	1
進來	jìnlái	to come in	进来	6
進去	jìnqù	to go in, to enter	进去	2
舊	jiù	old (nonliving thing), worn	旧	3
舊金山	Jiùjīnshān	San Francisco	旧金山	6

Traditonal	Pinyin	English	Simplified	Lesson
橘子	júzi	tangerine, mandarin	橘子	5
覺得	juéde	to feel	觉得	9
K 咖啡色	kāfēisè	brown	咖啡色	4
看	kàn	to look at, to see, to watch; to think	看	2, 4
看到	kàndào	to catch sight of, to see	看到	4
看看	kànkàn	to have a look	看看	4
看起來	kàn qǐlái	looks, impression or feeling of the look	看起来	4
可是	kěshì	but, however	可是	5
可以	kěyǐ	can, may	可以	1
刻	kè	a quarter (of an hour)	刻	2
客人	kèrén	guest	客人	8
客廳	kètīng	living room, lounge	客厅	3
空	kòng	free time, spare time	空	6
褲子	kùzi	trousers, pants	裤子	4
塊	kuài	[oral] monetary unit for dollar	块	5
快	kuài	nearly; fast, hurry	快	2
快樂	kuàilè	happy	快乐	1
寬	kuān	loose-fitting (clothing) (used in Taiwan); wide	宽	4
L 拉	lā	to pull	拉	7
啦	la	[exclamation]	啦	7
來	lái	[to invite someone to do something]; to come	来	1
來……	lái...	give me/us... (when ordering food)	来……	8
藍	lán	blue	蓝	4
老林	Lǎo Lín	Old Lin	老林	9
老王	Lǎo Wáng	Old Wang	老王	7
了	le	[grammatical word]	了	1
雷陣雨	léizhènyǔ	thunder shower	雷阵雨	9
冷	lěng	cold	冷	9
裡面	lǐmiàn	inside	里面	3
荔枝	lìzhī	lychee	荔枝	5
涼快	liángkuài	cool and pleasant	凉快	9
零	líng	zero	零	5
鈴	líng	(telephone ringing sound); bell	铃	7
令人	lìngrén	to make people..., to let people...	令人	9
另外	lìngwài	in addition, besides	另外	3
留	liú	to leave (a note); to keep	留	8 / 9
樓房	lóufáng	multistory building	楼房	3
錄影帶	lùyǐngdài	video, video cassette	录影带	6
綠色	lùsè	green	绿色	4
M 麻婆豆腐	mápó-dòufǔ	name of a hot and spicy bean curd dish	麻婆豆腐	8
馬上	mǎshàng	right away	马上	6
嘛	ma	[word ending - indicates an obvious situation]	嘛	4

Traditonal	Pinyin	English	Simplified	Lesson
買	mǎi	to buy	买	1
賣	mài	to sell	卖	5
慢	màn	slow	慢	2
慢走	màn zǒu	to walk slowly and take care	慢走	6
漫畫	mànhuà	comic books, comic strips, cartoons	漫画	2
毛	máo	[oral] 10-cent unit = 0.1 塊 kuài	毛	5
毛衣	máoyī	sweater	毛衣	4
帽子	màozi	hat, cap	帽子	5
沒問題	méi wèntí	no problems	没问题	7
每	měi	every	每	9
悶熱	mēnrè	sultry	闷热	9
門口	ménkǒu	doorway	门口	6
謎語	míyǔ	riddle	谜语	3
米飯	mǐfàn	plain rice	米饭	8
棉襖	mián'ǎo	cotton-padded coat	棉袄	4
明年	míngnián	next year	明年	1
明天	míngtiān	tomorrow	明天	1
母親	mǔqīn	mother	母亲	6
N 哪	nǎ	which, what	哪	1
哪裡	nǎlǐ	[oral] where	哪里	3
哪兒	nǎr	[oral] where	哪儿	3
哪位	nǎ/něi wèi	which one (person)	哪位	6
那	nà	[*conj.*] then; that	那	5
那麼	nàme	then	那么	1
男廁	náncè	men's restroom	男厕	7
念	niàn	to read	念	9
您	nín	[polite form] you	您	6
牛排	niúpái	steak	牛排	8
紐約	Niǔyuē	New York	纽约	6
暖和	nuǎnhuō	warm	暖和	9
女廁	nǚcè	women's restroom	女厕	7
O 喔	ō	[to express surprise/understanding] oh	喔	1
哦	ò	[to indicate realization] oh	哦	1
P 盤	pán	[*m.w.* - dish]; plate	盘	8
旁邊	pángbiān	the side	旁边	4
配	pèi	to match	配	4
皮鞋	píxié	leather shoes	皮鞋	4
篇	piān	[*m.w.* - short writing]	篇	10
便宜	piányí	cheap, inexpensive	便宜	5
漂亮	piàoliàng	pretty	漂亮	4
平常	píngcháng	usually	平常	8
平房	píngfáng	single-story house	平房	3
蘋果	píngguǒ	apple	苹果	5

Traditonal	Pinyin	English	Simplified	Lesson
破	pò	broken, torn	破	3
葡萄	pútáo	grapes	葡萄	5
Q 旗袍	qípáo	close-fitting dress with a high neck and slit skirt	旗袍	4
起床	qǐchuáng	to get up, to get out of bed	起床	2
氣溫	qìwēn	temperature	气温	9
錢	qián	money	钱	5
前面	qiánmiàn	front	前面	3
前年	qiánnián	the year before last	前年	1
前天	qiántiān	the day before yesterday	前天	1
淺	qiǎn	light (color); shallow	浅	4
晴	qíng	fine	晴	9
晴朗	qínglǎng	sunny, fine and cloudless	晴朗	9
晴天	qíngtiān	fine day, sunny day	晴天	9
請	qǐng	to invite; please	请	1
請進	qǐngjìn	come in please	请进	6
秋天	qiūtiān	autumn	秋天	9
去	qù	to go	去	1
去年	qùnián	last year	去年	1
裙子	qúnzi	skirt	裙子	4
R 熱	rè	hot	热	9
日	rì	day; the sun	日	1
日常	rìcháng	day-to-day, daily	日常	2
日記	rìjì	diary	日记	10
入口	rùkǒu	entrance	入口	7
S 沙發	shāfā	sofa (transliteration of sofa)	沙发	3
上	shàng	on top of, up; to go to; first part	上	3
上班	shàngbān	to go to work	上班	6
上(個)星期	shàng (ge) xīngqí	last week	上(个)星期	1
上個月	shàng ge yuè	last month	上个月	1
上面	shàngmiàn	above, on top of	上面	3
上午	shàngwǔ	morning	上午	2
上學	shàngxué	to go to school	上学	1
攝氏	shèshì	centigrade	摄氏	9
深	shēn	dark (color); deep	深	4
身心舒暢	shēnxīn-shūchàng	pleasant physically and mentally	身心舒畅	9
生	shēng	to be born, to give birth to; pupil	生	1
生活	shēnghuó	life	生活	2
生日	shēngrì	birthday	生日	1
詩	shī	poem	诗	9
獅子頭	shīzitóu	a dish of fried meatballs	狮子头	8
時候	shíhòu	time, moment	时候	1
時間	shíjiān	(concept of) time	时间	6
時髦	shímáo	fashion, fashionable	时髦	4

Traditonal	Pinyin	English	Simplified	Lesson
事	shì	thing, matter, business	事	6
市場	shìchǎng	market	市场	5
首	shǒu	[m.w. - poem]	首	9
瘦	shòu	tight-fitting (clothing), used in China; thin	瘦	4
書店	shūdiàn	bookshop	书店	5
書房	shūfáng	study	书房	3
舒服	shūfú	comfortable	舒服	4
叔叔	shúshu	[address] man of one's father's age; father's younger brother	叔叔	6
雙	shuāng	[m.w. - shoes, socks etc.] pair	双	4
雙胞胎	shuāngbāotāi	twins	双胞胎	1
水床	shuǐchuáng	water bed	水床	3
水果	shuǐguǒ	fruit	水果	5
睡	shuì	to sleep	睡	3
睡覺	shuìjiào	to sleep	睡觉	2
說	shuō	to say	说	6
說話	shuōhuà	to speak	说话	7
死	sǐ	deathly; dead, to die	死	9
送	sòng	to deliver, to send	送	3
送來	sòng lái	to deliver here	送来	3
送去	sòng qù	to send to	送去	3
酸	suān	sour	酸	5
酸辣湯	suānlàtāng	hot and sour soup	酸辣汤	8
隨便坐	suíbiàn zuò	sit anywhere	随便坐	8
所以	suǒyǐ	therefore	所以	8

T 台北	Táiběi	the capital city of R.O.C.	台北	9
太	tài	too (exceedingly)	太	3
太極拳	tàijíquán	taichi	太极拳	3
太太	tàitai	Mrs.; (in Taiwan) wife	太太	4
談	tán	to talk, to chat	谈	6
談話	tánhuà	to have a conversation, to talk, to chat	谈话	6
湯	tāng	soup	汤	8
討厭	tǎoyàn	annoying; to hate	讨厌	9
套	tào	[m.w. - clothing or furniture] set, suit	套	3
T恤	tīxù	T-shirt	T恤	4
添	tiān	to add	添	8
天空	tiānkōng	sky	天空	9
天哪！	tiān na!	Good heavens!	天哪！	3
天氣	tiānqì	weather	天气	9
甜	tián	sweet	甜	5
條	tiáo	[m.w. - trousers, shorts, skirt, river etc.]	条	4
跳舞	tiàowǔ	to dance	跳舞	2
聽	tīng	to listen, to hear	听	2
停	tíng	to stop	停	9
挺	tǐng	[oral] very	挺	4

Traditonal	Pinyin	English	Simplified	Lesson
同	tóng	same, together	同	1
同學	tóngxué	classmate, schoolmate	同学	6
推	tuī	to push	推	7
W 襪子	wàzi	socks	袜子	4
外面	wàimiàn	outside	外面	3
外套	wàitào	coat	外套	4
玩	wán	to play, to have fun	玩	6
碗	wǎn	[m.w. - rice, noodle soup etc.] bowl	碗	8
晚	wǎn	late, evening	晚	3
晚飯	wǎnfàn	dinner	晚饭	2
晚上	wǎnshàng	evening, night	晚上	2
王	Wáng; wáng	a surname; king	王	4
喂	wéi; wèi	hello (on the telephone); hey	喂	7
位	wèi	respectful measure word for people	位	6
味精	wèijīng	monosodium glutamate (M.S.G.)	味精	8
為什麼	wèishéme	why	为什么	6
問	wèn	to ask	问	6
我就是	wǒ jiùshì	I am (the person); speaking (on the phone)	我就是	7
臥室	wòshì	bedroom	卧室	3
午飯	wǔfàn	lunch	午饭	2
午後	wǔhòu	afternoon	午后	9
X 悉尼	Xīní	Sydney (used in China)	悉尼	6
西裝	xīzhuāng	Western-style attire, suit	西装	4
洗衣房	xǐyīfáng	laundry	洗衣房	3
洗衣機	xǐyījī	washing machine	洗衣机	3
矽谷	Xìgǔ	Silicon Valley	矽谷	6
下(個)星期	xià (ge) xīngqí	next week	下(个)星期	1
下個月	xià ge yuè	next month	下个月	1
下面	xiàmiàn	under, below	下面	3
下棋	xiàqí	to play chess	下棋	2
下午	xiàwǔ	afternoon	下午	2
下星期日	xià xīngqírì	next Sunday	下星期日	6
下雪	xiàxuě	to snow	下雪	9
下雨	xiàyǔ	to rain	下雨	9
夏天	xiàtiān	summer	夏天	9
先生	xiānshēng	Mr.; (in Taiwan) husband	先生	4
現在	xiànzài	now, at present	现在	2
香蕉	xiāngjiāo	banana	香蕉	5
想	xiǎng	to feel like; to think	想	5
小便	xiǎobiàn	to urinate; urine	小便	8
小弟弟	xiǎo dìdi	little boy	小弟弟	4
小姐	xiǎojiě	Miss; young lady	小姐	4
小妹妹	xiǎomèimei	little girl	小妹妹	4
小時	xiǎoshí	hour (time duration)	小时	6

Traditional	Pinyin	English	Simplified	Lesson
小王	Xiǎo Wáng	Little Wang	小王	9
小學	xiǎoxué	primary school	小学	6
笑話	xiàohuà	a joke	笑话	6
鞋子	xiézi	shoes	鞋子	3
寫	xiě	to write	写	2
寫下來	xiě xiàlái	to write down	写下来	6
新	xīn	new	新	3
星期	xīngqí	week	星期	1
星期二	xīngqí'èr	Tuesday	星期二	1
星期六	xīngqíliù	Saturday	星期六	1
星期日	xīngqírì	Sunday	星期日	1
星期三	xīngqísān	Wednesday	星期三	1
星期四	xīngqísì	Thursday	星期四	1
星期天	xīngqítiān	Sunday	星期天	1
星期五	xīngqíwǔ	Friday	星期五	1
星期一	xīngqíyī	Monday	星期一	1
行	xíng	all right, O.K.	行	1
修理	xiūlǐ	to repair, to fix	修理	3
雪梨	Xuělí	Sydney (used in Taiwan)	雪梨	6
Y 陽台	yángtái	balcony, veranda	阳台	3
洋房	yángfáng	Western-style house	洋房	3
洋裝	yángzhuāng	woman's dress	洋装	4
邀請	yāoqǐng	invitation, to invite	邀请	8
要	yào	to be going to;	要	1
		to want		5
也	yě	also	也	1
衣服	yīfú	clothes, clothing	衣服	4
醫生	yīshēng	doctor	医生	6
醫院	yīyuàn	hospital	医院	6
一共	yígòng	all together	一共	5
一下	yíxià	a short while	一下	6
一點都不	yìdiǎn dōu bù	not at all...	一点都不	5
一會兒	yìhuǐr	a little while	一会儿	7
一起	yìqǐ	together	一起	7
已經	yǐjīng	already	已经	2
以為	yǐwéi	thought (mistakenly)	以为	1
意思	yìsi	meaning	意思	9
陰天	yīntiān	cloudy day	阴天	9
因為	yīnwèi	because	因为	8
音樂	yīnyuè	music	音乐	2
銀行	yínháng	bank	银行	6
飲茶	yǐnchá	to have dimsum, a Cantonese meal of small snacks and tea	饮茶	8
游泳池	yóuyǒng chí	swimming pool	游泳池	3
尤其	yóuqí	especially	尤其	8

Traditonal	Pinyin	English	Simplified	Lesson
有時	yǒushí	sometimes	有时	9
有時候	yǒushíhòu	sometimes	有时候	8
又	yòu	again	又	9
右邊	yòubiān	right (location)	右边	3
預報	yùbào	forecast	预报	9
浴室	yùshì	bathroom, shower room	浴室	3
元	yuán	[formal] monetary unit for dollar	元	5
月	yuè	month; the moon	月	1
Z 雜誌	zázhì	magazine	杂志	5
在	zài	[indicates an action in progress];	在	2
		at, in, on		3
再	zài	again	再	6
糟糕	zāogāo	[oral] oh no, how terrible	糟糕	2
早	zǎo	early, morning	早	3
早飯	zǎofàn	breakfast	早饭	2
早上	zǎoshàng	(early) morning	早上	2
怎麼	zěme	how	怎么	4
怎麼回事	zěme huí shì	what happened, what's the matter	怎么回事	3
怎麼樣	zěmeyàng	how about, what about	怎么样	4
窄	zhǎi	tight-fitting (clothing) (used in Taiwan), narrow	窄	4
招待	zhāodài	to receive, reception	招待	6
找	zhǎo	to look for;	找	4
		to give change		5
找到了	zhǎodào le	found	找到了	4
找找	zhǎozhǎo	to have a look for	找找	4
隻	zhī	[m.w. - shoe, sock, animal]	只	4
只有	zhǐyǒu	only	只有	7
中國城	Zhōngguóchéng	Chinatown	中国城	7
中午	zhōngwǔ	midday, noon	中午	2
中學	zhōngxué	high school	中学	6
住	zhù	to live	住	6
紫	zǐ	purple	紫	4
字	zì	character, word	字	2
字典	zìdiǎn	dictionary	字典	5
自己	zìjǐ	self	自己	4
自己來	zìjǐ lái	to help oneself	自己来	8
走	zǒu	to leave, to go	走	6
最	zuì	the most	最	3
最低	zuìdī	lowest	最低	9
最高	zuìgāo	highest	最高	9
昨天	zuótiān	yesterday	昨天	1
左邊	zuǒbiān	left (location)	左边	3
左右	zuǒyòu	around	左右	7
坐	zuò	to sit	坐	6
做	zuò	to do, to make;	做	2
		to cook		8
做客	zuòkè	to be a guest	做客	9

Appendix 2

WORDS AND EXPRESSIONS
English-Chinese

English	Traditional	Pinyin
A		
a few days	幾天	jǐtiān
a little	(一)點	(yì)diǎn
a little while	一會(兒)	yìhuǐ(r)
a number of, some	一些	yìxiē
a quarter (of an hour)	一刻	yí kè
a short while	一下	yíxià
above, on top of	上面	shàngmiàn
action in progress	在	zài
afternoon	下午, 午後	xiàwǔ, wǔhòu
again	又, 再	yòu, zài
all	都	dōu
all right, O.K.	行	xíng
all together	一共	yígòng
already	已經	yǐjīng
also	也	yě
annoying; to hate	討厭	tǎoyàn
answer	回答	huídá
apple	蘋果	píngguǒ
around	左右	zuǒyòu
arrive late	遲到	chídào
ask	問	wèn
at, in, on	在	zài
autumn	秋天	qiūtiān
B		
bad; broken down	壞	huài
bag	袋	dài
balcony, veranda	陽台	yángtái
banana	香蕉	xiāngjiāo
bank	銀行	yínháng
bathroom, shower room	浴室	yùshì
be a guest	做客	zuòkè
be born; give birth to	生	shēng
because	因為	yīnwèi
bedroom	臥室	wòshì
behind	後面	hòumiàn
Beijing	北京	Běijīng
birthday	生日	shēngrì

English	Traditional	Pinyin
black	黑(色)	hēi(sè)
blue	藍(色)	lán(sè)
bookshop	書店	shūdiàn
breakfast	早飯	zǎofàn
broken down; bad	壞	huài
broken, torn	破	pò
brown	咖啡色	kāfēisè
but, however	但是, 可是	dànshì, kěshì
C		
can, may	可以	kěyǐ
car, vehicle	車子	chēzi
centigrade	攝氏	shèshì
character, word	字	zì
chat, to talk	談	tán
Chinatown	中國城	Zhōngguóchéng
Chinese-English dictionary	漢英字典	Hàn-Yīng zìdiǎn
Chinese soft shoes	功夫鞋	gōngfū xié
clothes, clothing	衣服	yīfú
cloudy	多雲	duōyún
cloudy day	陰天	yīntiān
coat	外套	wàitào
cold	冷	lěng
cold current	寒流	hánliú
come	來	lái
come back	回來	huílái
come in please	請進	qǐngjìn
come out	出來	chūlái
comfortable	舒服	shūfú
comic books, comic strips	漫畫	mànhuà
(completed action)	了	le
cook; do, make	做	zuò
cool and pleasant	涼快	liángkuài
correct	對	duì
cotton-padded coat	棉襖	mián'ǎo
D		
dance	跳舞	tiàowǔ
dark (color); deep	深	shēn
date; number	號	hào

English	Traditional	Pinyin	English	Traditional	Pinyin
day; the sun	日	rì	feel like; think	想	xiǎng
day after tomorrow	後天	hòutiān	feel with the wearing	穿起來	chuān qǐlái
day before yesterday	前天	qiántiān	fine and cloudless	晴朗	qínglǎng
deathly; dead, die	死	sǐ	fine day, sunny day	晴天	qíngtiān
deep; dark (color)	深	shēn	finish classes	放學	fàngxué
deliver, send	送	sòng	fish (v.)	釣魚	diàoyú
deliver here	送來	sòng lái	fix, repair	修理	xiūlǐ
department store	百貨公司	bǎihuò gōngsī	flats, units	公寓	gōngyù
dictionary	字典	zìdiǎn	floor	地板	dìbǎn
die	死	sǐ	forecast	預報	yùbào
differ from	差	chā	found	找到了	zhǎodào le
dining room	飯廳	fàntīng	free time, spare time	空	kòng
dinner	晚飯	wǎnfàn	Friday	星期五	xīngqíwǔ
disturb, to trouble	打擾	dǎrǎo	front	前面	qiánmiàn
do	做	zuò	fruit	水果	shuǐguǒ
doctor	醫生	yīshēng			
don't be formal, make yourself at home	別客氣	bié kèqì	**G**		
			garage	車庫	chēkù
doorway	門口	ménkǒu	garden	花園	huāyuán
dot	點	diǎn	get up, get out of bed	起床	qǐchuáng
dress - close fitting with a high neck and slit skirt	旗袍	qípáo	give	給	gěi
			give birth to; be born	生	shēng
E			give change	找	zhǎo
early	早	zǎo	give us... (ordering food)	來……	lái...
eat	吃	chī	go	去	qù
entrance	入口	rùkǒu	go home	回家	huíjiā
especially	尤其	yóuqí	go in, enter	進去	jìnqù
evening, night	晚上	wǎnshàng	go out	出去	chūqù
everyone	大家	dàjiā	go to	上	shàng
(exclam. - realization)	哦	ò	go to school	上學	shàngxué
(exclam. - surprise; understanding)	喔	ō	go to work	上班	shàngbān
			go to, arrive	到	dào
excrement	大便	dàbiàn	going to, want	要	yào
exit	出口	chūkǒu	Good heavens!	天哪！	tiān na!
expensive	貴	guì	good-looking	好看	hǎokàn
extremely	非常	fēicháng	grapes	葡萄	pútáo
			green	綠(色)	lù(sè)
F			guess	猜	cāi
Fahrenheit	華氏	huáshì	guest	客人	kèrén
fashion, fashionable	時髦	shímáo			
fast; hurry	快	kuài	**H**		
fat	肥	féi	half	半	bàn
father	父親	fùqīn	happy	高興,	gāoxìng,
father's younger brother	叔叔	shúshu		快樂	kuàilè
feel	覺得	juéde	hat, cap	帽子	màozi
			hate; annoying	討厭	tǎoyàn

English	Traditional	Pinyin
have a conversation, chat	談話	tánhuà
have a look	看看	kànkàn
have a look for	找找	zhǎozhǎo
have a meal	吃飯	chīfàn
have bad luck	倒霉	dǎoméi
have dimsum	飲茶	yǐnchá
have tea	喝茶	hē chá
hello (on the phone); hey	喂	wéi; wèi
help oneself	自己來	zìjǐ lái
high school	中學	zhōngxué
highest	最高	zuìgāo
homework	功課	gōngkè
hospital	醫院	yīyuàn
hot	熱	rè
hot and sour soup	酸辣湯	suānlàtāng
hour (time duration)	小時	xiǎoshí
house	房子	fángzi
how	怎麼	zěme
how about, what about	怎麼樣	zěmeyàng
how hot	多熱	duó rè
how much, how many	多少	duōshǎo
however, but	但是, 可是	dànshì, kěshì
husband (in Taiwan); Mr.	先生	xiānshēng

I

English	Traditional	Pinyin
I am (the person); speaking	我就是	wǒ jiù shì
in addition, besides	另外	lìngwài
in, at, on	在	zài
incorrect	錯	cuò
inside	裡面	lǐmiàn
introduce	介紹	jièshào
invitation, to invite	邀請	yāoqǐng
invite; please	請	qǐng

J

English	Traditional	Pinyin
just, happen to	剛好	gānghǎo

K

English	Traditional	Pinyin
keep	留	liú
king; a surname	王	wáng; Wáng
kitchen	廚房	chúfáng
kite	風箏	fēngzhēng

L

English	Traditional	Pinyin
last month	上個月	shàng ge yuè
last week	上(個)星期	shàng (ge) xīngqí

English	Traditional	Pinyin
last year	去年	qùnián
late, evening	晚	wǎn
laundry	洗衣房	xǐyīfáng
leather shoes	皮鞋	píxié
leave (a note)	留	liú
leave, go	走	zǒu
left (location)	左邊	zuǒbiān
let off, let go, release	放	fàng
life	生活	shēnghuó
light (color); shallow	淺	qiǎn
listen, hear	聽	tīng
little boy	小弟弟	xiǎo dìdi
little girl	小妹妹	xiǎo mèimei
Little Wang	小王	Xiǎo Wáng
live	住	zhù
living room	客廳	kètīng
long	長	cháng
look at, see, watch	看	kàn
look for	找	zhǎo
looks	看起來	kàn qǐlái
loose-fitting (clothing)	寬	kuān (in Taiwan)
	肥	féi (in China)
lowest	最低	zuìdī
lunch	午飯	wǔfàn
lychee	荔枝	lìzhī

M

English	Traditional	Pinyin
m.w. - book, magazine	本	běn
m.w. - clothing, affair	件	jiàn
m.w. - clothing, furniture (set)	套	tào
m.w. - dish (plate)	盤	pán
m.w. - grapes, bananas (bunch)	串	chuàn
m.w. - hat, cap	頂	dǐng
m.w. - newspaper, copy	份	fèn
m.w. - poem	首	shǒu
m.w. - rice, soup (bowl)	碗	wǎn
m.w. - room	間	jiān
m.w. - shoe, sock, animal	隻	zhī
m.w. - shoes, socks (pair)	雙	shuāng
m.w. - trousers, skirt	條	tiáo
magazine	雜誌	zázhì
make	做	zuò
make people...	令人	lìngrén
man of one's father's age (*address*)	叔叔	shúshu
map	地圖	dìtú
market	市場	shìchǎng

English	Traditional	Pinyin
match (v.)	配	pèi
matter, business, thing	事	shì
may, can	可以	kěyǐ
meaning	意思	yìsi
meatballs (fried, or cooked with Chinese cabbage)	獅子頭	shīzitóu
men's restroom	男廁	náncè
menu	菜單	càidān
midday, noon	中午	zhōngwǔ
midnight	半夜	bànyè
minute	分	fēn
Miss; young lady	小姐	xiǎojiě
Monday	星期一	xīngqíyī
monetary unit - cent	分	fēn
10 cents	角	jiǎo
10 cents [oral]	毛	máo
dollar	元 (圓)	yuán
dollar [oral]	塊	kuài
money	錢	qián
M.S.G.	味精	wèijīng
month	月	yuè
more, a lot	多	duō
morning	上午	shàngwǔ
morning (early)	早上	zǎoshàng
most	最	zuì
mother	母親	mǔqīn
mother's sister (in China)	姨	yí
(in Taiwan)	阿姨	āyí
movie	電影	diànyǐng
Mr.; husband	先生	xiānshēng
Mrs.; wife	太太	tàitai
multi-story building	樓房	lóufáng

N

English	Traditional	Pinyin
nearly; fast; hurry	快	kuài
new	新	xīn
New York	紐約	Niǔyuē
newspaper	報紙	bàozhǐ
next month	下個月	xià ge yuè
next Sunday	下星期日	xià xīngqírì
next week	下(個)星期	xià (ge) xīngqí
next year	明年	míngnián
night, evening	晚上	wǎnshàng
no problems	沒問題	méi wèntí
not at all...	一點都不	yìdiǎn dōu bù
not bad, pretty good [oral]	還不錯	hái búcuò

English	Traditional	Pinyin
not being courteous; not at all, you're welcome	不客氣	bú kèqì
now, at present	現在	xiànzài
number	號碼	hàomǎ
number; date	號	hào

O

English	Traditional	Pinyin
o'clock; dot	點	diǎn
often	常, 常常	cháng, chángcháng
oh (surprise, understanding)	喔	ō
oh (realization)	哦	ò
oh no, how terrible [oral]	糟糕	zāogāo
old (nonliving things), worn	舊	jiù
Old Lin	老林	Lǎo Lín
Old Wang	老王	Lǎo Wáng
on top of, above	上面	shàngmiàn
on, at, in	在	zài
one's heart's content	過癮	guòyǐn
only	只有	zhǐyǒu
opposite (location)	對面	duìmiàn
or	還是	háishì
orange (color)	橙色	chéngsè
order the food	點菜	diǎncài
outside	外面	wàimiàn

P

English	Traditional	Pinyin
pair [measure word]	雙	shuāng
pick (someone) up	接	jiē
pineapple (in China)	菠蘿,	bōluó,
(in Taiwan)	鳳梨	fènglí
plain rice (in China)	米飯,	mǐfàn,
(in Taiwan)	白飯	báifàn
play chess	下棋	xiàqí
play; to dial	打	dǎ
play, to have fun	玩	wán
pleasant physically and mentally	身心舒暢	shēnxīn-shūchàng
please; invite	請	qǐng
plum; a surname	李	lí; Lǐ
poem	詩	shī
pretty	漂亮	piàoliàng
primary school	小學	xiǎoxué
probably	大概	dàgài
pull	拉	lā
purple	紫(色)	zǐ (sè)

English	Traditional	Pinyin
push	推	tuī
put	放	fàng

Q

English	Traditional	Pinyin
queen	皇后	huánghòu

R

English	Traditional	Pinyin
rain (v.)	下雨	xiàyǔ
read	念	niàn
receive, reception	招待	zhāodài
red	紅(色)	hóng(sè)
refrigerator	冰箱,	bīngxiāng,
	電冰箱	diànbīngxiāng
repair, fix	修理	xiūlǐ
restaurant	飯館,	fànguǎn,
	餐館,	cānguǎn,
	館子	guǎnzi
restroom	廁所,洗手間	cèsuǒ, xǐshǒujiān
return, come back	回來	huílái
rice (cooked)	飯	fàn
riddle	謎語	míyǔ
right (location)	右邊	yòubiān
right away	馬上	mǎshàng
right, correct	對	duì

S

English	Traditional	Pinyin
same, together	同	tóng
San Francisco	舊金山	Jiùjīnshān
Saturday	星期六	xīngqíliù
say	說	shuō
school work, homework	功課	gōngkè
season	季	jì
send	送	sòng
see, catch sight of	見	jiàn
seem, be like	好像	hǎoxiàng
self	自己	zìjǐ
sell	賣	mài
send to	送去	sòng qù
serve the rice	盛飯	chéng fàn
set, suit (m.w.)	套	tào
settle accounts	結帳	jiézhàng
shirt	襯衫	chènshān
shoes	鞋子	xiézi
short (length)	短	duǎn
shorts	短褲	duǎnkù
should	該	gāi
side	旁邊	pángbiān

English	Traditional	Pinyin
(sigh)	唉	ài
Silicon Valley	矽谷	Xìgǔ
simple meal [modest form]	便飯	biànfàn
sing	唱歌	chànggē
single-story house	平房	píngfáng
sit	坐	zuò
sit anywhere	隨便坐	suíbiàn zuò
skirt	裙子	qúnzi
sky	天空	tiānkōng
sleep	睡, 睡覺	shuì, shuìjiào
slow	慢	màn
snow (v.)	下雪	xiàxuě
socks	襪子	wàzi
some other day	改天	gǎitiān
sometimes	有時,	yǒushí,
	有時候	yǒushíhòu
soup	湯	tāng
sour	酸	suān
spare time	空	kòng
speak	說, 說話	shuō, shuōhuà
spring	春天	chūntiān
spring rolls	春捲	chūnjuǎn
steak	牛排	niúpái
still	還	hái
stop	停	tíng
strawberry	草莓	cǎoméi
streaming with sweat	汗流浹背	hànliú-jiábèi
street	街	jiē
study (n.)	書房	shūfáng
sultry	悶熱	mēnrè
summer	夏天	xiàtiān
Sunday	星期日,	xīngqírì,
	星期天	xīngqítiān
sunny	晴朗	qínglǎng
sunny day	晴天	qíngtiān
sweater	毛衣	máoyī
sweet	甜	tián
sweet and sour pork	咕咾肉,	gūlǎoròu,
	咕嚕肉	gūlūròu
swimming pool	游泳池	yóuyǒng chí
Sydney (used in China)	悉尼,	Xīní,
(used in Taiwan)	雪梨	Xuělí

T

English	Traditional	Pinyin
taichi	太極拳	tàijíquán
take to	帶去	dài qù

English	Traditional	Pinyin
talk; chat	談	tán
tangerine	橘子	júzi
teach (at school)	教書	jiāoshū
telephone	電話	diànhuà
telephone ringing sound	鈴	líng
television	電視	diànshì
television set	電視機	diànshìjī
temperature	氣溫	qìwēn
that's enough	好了好了	hǎo le hǎo le
then	那，那麼	nà, nàme
therefore	所以	suǒyǐ
thin, skinny	瘦	shòu
thought (mistakenly)	以為	yǐwéi
thunder shower	雷陣雨	léizhènyǔ
Thursday	星期四	xīngqísì
tight-fitting (clothing)	窄	zhǎi (in Taiwan)
	瘦	shòu (in China)
time - concept	時間	shíjiān
time, moment	時候	shíhòu
to, until	到	dào
today	今天	jīntiān
together	一起	yìqǐ
tomorrow	明天	míngtiān
too (exceedingly)	太	tài
torn, broken	破	pò
trousers, pants	褲子	kùzi
T-shirt	T恤	tīxù
Tuesday	星期二	xīngqí'èr
twins	雙胞胎	shuāngbāotāi

U

English	Traditional	Pinyin
under, below	下面	xiàmiàn
university	大學	dàxué
urinate, urine	小便	xiǎobiàn
usually	平常	píngcháng

V

English	Traditional	Pinyin
vehicle, car	車子	chēzi
very [oral]	挺	tǐng
video, video cassette	錄影帶	lùyǐngdài
visit	拜訪	bàifǎng

W

English	Traditional	Pinyin
w.e. - obvious situation	嘛	ma
wait	等	děng
want; be going to	要	yào
warm	暖和	nuǎnhuō
washing machine	洗衣機	xǐyījī

English	Traditional	Pinyin
watch (timepiece)	錶	biǎo
water bed	水床	shuǐchuáng
wear (clothes, shoes etc.)	穿	chuān
weather	天氣	tiānqì
Wednesday	星期三	xīngqísān
week	星期	xīngqí
weight - a unit	斤	jīn
= 0.6 kg in Taiwan = 0.5 kg in China		
well-fitting (clothing)	合身	héshēn
Western-style attire, suit	西裝	xīzhuāng
what happened, what's the matter	怎麼回事	zěme huí shì
what time	幾點鐘	jǐ diǎn zhōng
where	哪裡, 哪兒	nǎlǐ, nǎr
which one (person)	哪位	nǎ/něi wèi
which, what	哪	nǎ
white	白(色)	bái(sè)
White House	白宮	Báigōng
why	為什麼	wèishéme
wife (used in Taiwan)	太太	tàitai
will; can, be ble to	會	huì
wind	風	fēng
windy	刮風	guāfēng
winter	冬天	dōngtiān
wish	祝	zhù
woman of one's mother's age (address)	阿姨	āyí
woman's dress (in China)	連衣裙，	liányīqún,
(in Taiwan)	洋裝	yángzhuāng
women's restroom	女廁	nǚcè
word, character	字	zì
work, to work	工作	gōngzuò
worn	舊	jiù
write	寫	xiě
write down	寫下來	xiě xiàlái
wrong, incorrect	錯	cuò

Y

English	Traditional	Pinyin
yellow	黃(色)	huáng(sè)
yesterday	昨天	zuótiān
you [polite form]	您	nín

Z

English	Traditional	Pinyin
zero	零	líng

Answers to the riddles on page 40:
1. 天 2. 星 3. 早 4. 字

Appendix 3

LEARN TO WRITE
by lesson

	Chinese		English
1	月	yuè	month; the moon
	日	rì	day; the sun
	號	hào	date; number
	今	jīn	present (time)
	明	míng	bright
	昨	zuó	yesterday
	天	tiān	day; sky
	星	xīng	star
	期	qí	a period of time
	對	duì	right, correct
	錯	cuò	wrong, incorrect
	可	kě	may, approve
	以	yǐ	to use
	行	xíng	all right; O.K.; to walk
	生	shēng	to be born, to give birth to; student
2	在	zài	[in progress]; at, on, in
	做	zuò	to do, to make
	看	kàn	to read, to look at, to watch
	書	shū	book
	寫	xiě	to write
	字	zì	character, word
	現	xiàn	now, present
	點	diǎn	o'clock; dot
	分	fēn	minute; cent
	半	bàn	half
	了	le	[grammatical word]
	下	xià	latter part; under
	午	wǔ	noon, midday
	早	zǎo	early; morning
	晚	wǎn	late; evening, night
3	哪	nǎ	where, which, what
	兒	ér	[word ending]; son
	前	qián	front, before
	面	miàn	[word ending - location]; face

	Chinese		English
	後	hòu	behind, after
	右	yòu	right (location)
	邊	biān	[word ending - location]; side
	左	zuǒ	left (location)
	裡	lǐ	inside
	外	wài	outside
	回	huí	to return; [measure word]
	來	lái	to come
	怎	zě	how
	事	shì	business, matter
	見	jiàn	to see
4	穿	chuān	to wear
	衣	yī	clothes
	服	fú	clothes
	先	xiān	first
	太	tài	too (exceedingly)
	黑	hēi	black
	白	bái	white
	紅	hóng	red
	黃	huáng	yellow
	藍	lán	blue
	綠	lù	green
	色	sè	color
	件	jiàn	[measure word for clothes]
	呢	ne	[question word]
	找	zhǎo	to look for
5	多	duō	many, much, more
	少	shǎo	few, little, less
	錢	qián	money
	買	mǎi	to buy
	賣	mài	to sell
	塊	kuài	dollar
	毛	máo	10-cent unit
	到	dào	to arrive, to go to

Chinese		English
樣	yàng	appearance
還	hái	also, still
要	yào	to want; to be going to
給	gěi	to give
謝	xiè	to thank
本	běn	[measure word for books, magazines etc.]
共	gòng	together

6

Chinese		English
空	kòng	free time
玩	wán	to play, to have fun
住	zhù	to live
電	diàn	electricity
話	huà	speech
請	qǐng	please; to invite
問	wèn	to ask
進	jìn	to enter
等	děng	to wait
出	chū	to go/come out
時	shí	time, hour
間	jiān	within (time/space); [measure word for room]
該	gāi	should
走	zǒu	to go, to leave, to walk
再	zài	again

7

Chinese		English
偉	wěi	great
蘭	lán	orchid
起	qǐ	to rise
您	nín	[polite form] you
李	Lǐ; lǐ	a surname; plum
位	wèi	[measure word for person]
叔	shú	one's father's younger brother
候	hòu	time
游	yóu	to swim
泳	yǒng	swim
城	chéng	town
雙	shuāng	pair

Chinese		English
功	gōng	skill, effort
夫	fū	man
鞋	xié	shoes

8

Chinese		English
因	yīn	cause, reason
為	wèi	for
所	suǒ	so; place
常	cháng	often, usually
館	guǎn	shop, building
子	zi; zǐ	[suffix]; son, child
飲	yǐn	to drink
茶	chá	tea
都	dōu	all
平	píng	flat, even
客	kè	guest
氣	qì	manner; air
湯	tāng	soup
炒	chǎo	to stir-fry
得	de	[degree, result of]

9

Chinese		English
雨	yǔ	rain
雪	xuě	snow
刮	guā	to blow (wind)
風	fēng	wind
熱	rè	hot
冷	lěng	cold
涼	liáng	cool
春	chūn	spring
夏	xià	summer
秋	qiū	autumn, fall
冬	dōng	winter
台	tái	platform, Taiwan
北	běi	north
暖	nuǎn	warm
陰	yīn	cloudy
晴	qíng	sunny
最	zuì	the most
高	gāo	high
低	dī	low
度	dù	degree